WALKING

DALES WAY

HILLSIDE GUIDES - ACROSS THE NORTH

Long Distance Walks
- COAST TO COAST WALK
- DALES WAY
- CUMBRIA WAY
- WESTMORLAND WAY
- FURNESS WAY
- NIDDERDALE WAY
- BRONTE WAY
- CALDERDALE WAY
- PENDLE WAY

Hillwalking - Lake District
- LAKELAND FELLS - SOUTH
- LAKELAND FELLS - EAST
- LAKELAND FELLS - NORTH
- LAKELAND FELLS - WEST

Circular Walks - Yorkshire Dales
- WHARFEDALE
- MALHAMDALE
- SWALEDALE
- NIDDERDALE
- THREE PEAKS
- WENSLEYDALE
- HOWGILL FELLS
- HARROGATE & WHARFE VALLEY
- RIPON & LOWER WENSLEYDALE

Circular Walks - Lancashire/North West
- BOWLAND
- PENDLE & THE RIBBLE
- LUNESDALE
- WEST PENNINE MOORS
- ARNSIDE & SILVERDALE

Circular Walks - North Pennines
- EDEN VALLEY
- ALSTON & ALLENDALE

Circular Walks - North/East Yorkshire
- NORTH YORK MOORS, SOUTHERN
- HOWARDIAN HILLS

Circular Walks - South Pennines
- ILKLEY MOOR
- BRONTE COUNTRY
- CALDERDALE

Short Scenic Walks
Yorkshire Dales
- UPPER WHARFEDALE
- LOWER WHARFEDALE
- MALHAMDALE
- UPPER WENSLEYDALE
- LOWER WENSLEYDALE
- SWALEDALE
- NIDDERDALE
- SEDBERGH & DENTDALE
- RIBBLESDALE
- INGLETON & WESTERN DALES

Northern England
- HARROGATE & KNARESBOROUGH
- ILKLEY & WASHBURN VALLEY
- AIRE VALLEY
- AMBLESIDE & LANGDALE
- BORROWDALE
- BOWLAND
- AROUND PENDLE
- RIBBLE VALLEY
- HAWORTH
- HEBDEN BRIDGE

*Send for a detailed current catalogue and price list
and also visit www.hillsidepublications.co.uk*

WALKING COUNTRY

———

DALES WAY

Paul Hannon

———

Hillside

HILLSIDE
PUBLICATIONS
20 Wheathead Crescent
Keighley
West Yorkshire
BD22 6LX

First published 1988
Reprinted 6 times including 1997 revision
Fully Revised 2012 edition

ISBN 978-1-907626-10-4

Cover illustration: River Wharfe at Bolton Abbey
Back cover: Crook of Lune; Dent; above Grassington
Page 1: Langstrothdale
Page 3: Kettlewell
Page 5: Yockenthwaite stone circle
(Paul Hannon/Hillslides Picture Library)

The sketch maps in this book are based upon
1947 Ordnance Survey One-Inch maps

Printed by Steffprint
Unit 5, Keighley Industrial Park
Royd Ings Avenue
Keighley
West Yorkshire
BD21 4DZ

CONTENTS

MAPS COVERING THE WALK

Ordnance Survey Landranger (1:50,000 scale) •97•98•104

Ordnance Survey Explorer (1:25,000 scale) •OL2•OL7•OL19•OL30•297

Harvey Maps (1:40,000 scale) ₴Dales Way

INTRODUCTION

The Dales Way is an 80-mile long-distance walk from Ilkley to Bowness-on-Windermere, passing through the heart of the Yorkshire Dales. Arriving on the scene in the late 1960s, it was the brainchild of members of the West Riding group of the Ramblers' Association, who could envisage the unquestionable appeal of a through route from the edge of the West Riding conurbations to the very shore of the country's largest lake. The idea of following rivers through the Dales results in a very well-defined route through Wharfedale and Dentdale: the rivers Lune and Kent then chip in with a few miles during a crossing of undulating hills into the heart of Lakeland.

An enterprising feature of those early plans was the addition of link paths guiding footsteps from larger towns and cities to the main route, and thereby further promoting the opportunities to walk out of the grime and into the green. These links are also fully described within this guide. A link with other long-distance routes was established with the arrival of the Ebor Way, a 70-mile walk between Ilkley and Helmsley, start of the Cleveland Way.

The terrain of Dales Way country makes for a less demanding walk than many of the long-distance paths, which has boosted its popularity as a good choice for a first ever multi-day walk. Whilst it is largely a riverside route inside the Yorkshire Dales, the Way still takes opportunity to gain height along the valley sides of both Wharfedale and Dentdale, thus adding variety and more extensive views. Even down on the banks of the rivers one can usually enjoy distant vistas thanks to the surround of high fells.

In the valleys many settlements are encountered, all delight-fully individual places. Though most profuse in Wharfedale, which includes showpieces such as Kettlewell and Burnsall, wonderful Dent manages to equal anything before or after it. Throughout the walk one is never far from some feature of architectural or historic interest, including stone circle, Roman road, romantic abbey, 14th century fortified manor house, 15th century shooting lodge and 17th century Quaker meeting house. Add to this a wealth of churches and bridges with, not surprisingly, the latter being most diverse. From packhorse bridge to suspension bridge, and Victorian viaduct to concrete motorway bridge, the Dales Way finds them all.

From Ilkley through to Bowness the Dales Way - with very few reservations - takes you through scenery of the highest order, and though many will have already experienced the beauty of Wharfedale, far fewer will be aware of the delights awaiting beyond, so savour the Dee, Lune and Kent!

THE DALES WAY

80 miles from Ilkley to Bowness

Windermere
BOWNESS
Staveley
Burneside
Grayrigg

*LAKE
DISTRICT*

National Parks

Kendal
Lowgill

Sedbergh
Millthrop
Dent
Cowgill

*YORKSHIRE
DALES*

Gearstones

Milestone at Gearstones

Manor House, Ilkley

Oughtershaw
Yockenthwaite
Hubberholme
Buckden
Starbotton
Kettlewell

Conistone

Grassington
Linton
Burnsall Hebden

Appletreewick
Bolton Abbey

Addingham
ILKLEY

Planning the Walk

The Dales Way's 80 miles fit comfortably into a week's walk, giving an average distance of 13 to 14 miles over six days. The main route has been divided into that number of self-contained stages, each with essential information and a simple sketch map preceding a detailed route description. Notes on features along the way are dovetailed between in italics in order to ensure the most important description can be easily viewed while still locating all the relevant features of interest.

Obviously some will wish to vary their stages to lengthen or shorten certain days, or to fit in with specific accommodation needs. All but one of these stages end somewhere with some accommodation choices. Stage 3 uses Gearstones as a stepping-off point with limited options: Ribblehead, with inn and station, is a long mile to the west, or you should be able to catch/arrange a lift along the B6255 to Hawes, Ingleton or Horton, with ample accommodation. If you've stayed higher up Wharfedale than Buckden you should be able to cross into Dentdale, where you'll need to get as far as Cowgill for the night. Another option would be to split Stages 4 and 5 into three days: this gives you 10 miles to Dent, 8^3_4 miles to Lincoln's Inn Bridge (for bus/lift/taxi into Sedbergh), and then 12^1_2 miles from the bridge to Burneside.

A very useful and inexpensive tool is the Dales Way Handbook, produced annually by the Ramblers' Association West Riding Area and the Dales Way Association. It contains a wealth of information including transport and accommodation details. The walk's very popularity can cause accommodation problems: if possible consider starting on a midweek day, thus avoiding the logjam effect of everybody arriving at the same village on the same night, chasing the same beds! Several firms carry groaning rucksacks to and from locations along the route, leaving you to enjoy long days with a light daypack – a very useful addition to the holiday experience: some will organise your entire trip for you too.

Another useful feature of the Dales Way is the availability of public transport to and from its extremities, with both being at the terminus of a railway line. Ilkley is served from Bradford and Leeds, while Windermere (just 1^1_2 miles from Bowness) is served from Lancaster. Both also have good bus services to the outside world.

The path itself is generally in very good condition, with the first half through Wharfedale being the easiest to follow. The remote section beyond Sedbergh is, in marked contrast, only rarely visited, and consequently there is little evidence of any previous walkers. However, waymarking, much initiated by the Dales Way Association, has greatly eased navigation.

SOME USEFUL FACILITIES

A general guide: the only thing that might not change overnight is the location of a railway station! (a Post office is usually, but not always, a shop as well, while a bus could be just once a day)

	Hotel/B&B	Hostel/Barn	Camping	Bus service	Rail station	Pub	Post office	Shop	WC	Phone box	Cafe
Ilkley	•			•	•	•	•	•	•	•	•
Addingham	•		•	•		•	•	•	•	•	•
Bolton Bridge	•			•		•					•
Bolton Abbey	•			•		•	•		•	•	•
Cavendish Pavilion							•	•			•
Barden			•							•	
Howgill	•		•	•						•	
Appletreewick	•		•	•		•				•	
Burnsall	•			•		•	•	•	•	•	•
Hebden	•			•		•			•	•	•
Linton	•			•		•			•	•	
Grassington	•			•		•	•	•	•	•	•
Kettlewell	•	•		•		•	•	•	•	•	•
Starbotton	•			•		•			•		
Buckden	•			•		•		•	•	•	•
Hubberholme	•	•				•					
Yockenthwaite	•										
Beckermonds	•		•								
Oughtershaw	•	•								•	
Gearstones/Ribblehd	•	•			•	•					
Stone House/Cowgill	•		•	•	•	•				•	
Dent	•		•	•		•	•	•	•	•	•
Sedbergh	•		•	•		•	•	•	•	•	•
Lincoln's Inn Bridge			•								
Howgill	•									•	
Lowgill										•	
Grayrigg	•		•	•						•	
Skelsmergh/A6	•		•								
Kendal	•	•		•	•	•	•	•	•	•	•
Burneside	•		•	•	•			•	•		
Bowston	•		•			•				•	
Staveley	•			•	•	•	•	•	•	•	•
Bowness	•		•	•		•	•	•	•	•	•
Windermere	•	•		•	•	•	•	•	•	•	•

ILKLEY TO BURNSALL

DISTANCE *12 miles (19km)*   ASCENT *500ft (150m)*

ORDNANCE SURVEY MAPS
1:50,000
Landranger 98 - Wensleydale & Upper Wharfedale
Landranger 104 - Leeds, Bradford & Harrogate
1:25,000
Explorer 297 - Lower Wharfedale & Washburn Valley
Explorer OL2 - Yorkshire Dales South/West

The opening stage of the Dales Way is reserved almost exclusively for the riverbank, more so than any of the days ahead. As a result the walking is very easy, and the surroundings happily still manage to vary enormously. Several villages tempt very short detours from the Wharfe. Though Bolton Priory may be the highlight, Burnsall is a lovely spot to finish a day's walking.

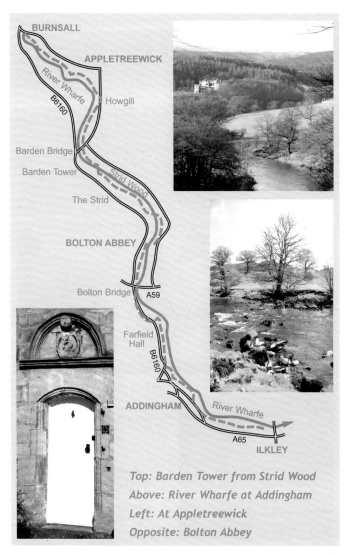

BURNSALL

APPLETREEWICK

River Wharfe

B6160

Howgill

Barden Bridge

Barden Tower

Strid Wood

The Strid

BOLTON ABBEY

Bolton Bridge   A59

Farfield Hall

B6160

ADDINGHAM   River Wharfe

A65

ILKLEY

Top: Barden Tower from Strid Wood
Above: River Wharfe at Addingham
Left: At Appletreewick
Opposite: Bolton Abbey

Ilkley is the highest town on the Wharfe, a perfect stepping-stone between industrial conurbations downstream and the joys of the Yorkshire Dales immediately upstream. This thriving town blends a workaday existence with that of a tourist venue, as shops, pubs and cafes line spacious streets draped in a tapestry of floral colour. From Ilkley's bustling pavements eyes are drawn to the moorland high above: this brooding mass of heather and gritstone exerts a powerful influence, and one is almost literally drawn up to its airy heights. Many of Ilkley Moor's finest features are seen during the final stages of the Bradford and Leeds link routes.

All Saints church has a 500-year old tower, but is best known for its Anglo-Saxon crosses: seek out also a well-preserved effigy of a 14th century knight, Adam de Middleton. The church covers part of the site of the Roman fort of Olicana: built around 79 AD, it sat astride a crossroads of ways linking Ribchester, York, Manchester and Aldborough, near Boroughbridge. Evidence is restricted to a small section of preserved wall. Also by the church is the fine 16th century Manor House, a museum of local interest.

The Old Bridge, Ilkley

First steps along the River Wharfe

The Dales Way begins at the Old Bridge on the Wharfe, gained by turning down New Brook Street from the parish church. Before the modern road bridge, descend to trace the river upstream to the Old Bridge. *Alongside is the first of several Dales Way information panels along the route, as well as a stone seat whose twin you will encounter at the other end of the walk.* Without crossing the shapely bridge, the Dales Way kicks off by heading upstream on a surfaced path past a garden centre, soon joining a tennis club drive. Bear round to the buildings then break off to a kissing-gate on the left. A path heads off through half a dozen pastures linked by kissing-gates. The river is rejoined in woodland, then at the end of a grassy pasture you are nudged onto a quiet back road. *This is the old road running parallel with the A65 Ilkley-Skipton road.*

Head along the roadside footway in company with the river, and leave at the first chance on Old Lane, the access road to Low Mill Village. *This is an interesting arrangement of a former mill site. Castleberg Scar climbs high above the opposite bank of the river.* Forge on between the houses and onto an enclosed way, soon becoming a back road on the edge of Addingham. When level with the parish church take a little path down steps to an arched foot-bridge en route to the church, and officially the path enters the churchyard. *St Peter's notable features include its oak roof, Saxon cross, and examples of the carved 'mouse' trademark of the Kilburn workshops.*

Leave on the church drive, but without descending to cross a bridge, instead bear right to a footbridge between houses. This narrow way quickly emerges onto North Street. *Addingham was the scene of a thousand-strong Luddite riot in 1826, an abortive attempt to break into the mill to smash the power looms. Despite a 1991 by-pass, Addingham's long main street retains much of its bustle, with pubs and shops.*

St Peter's church, Addingham

River Wharfe above Addingham

Unless seeking the village centre turn right along North Street, and just past a small green a path drops to a suspension footbridge on the Wharfe. Don't cross but turn upstream on a pleasant path, keeping with the river at a fork. High Mill - another assortment of modern homes - soon deflects you briefly from the river, through its courtyard and ahead to the drive into a caravan park: only a short way in, a path returns to the Wharfe alongside a weir. The river leads unfailingly up-dale, interrupted by a steep, wooded bank before dropping back to the Wharfe. After several further pastures you climb to the road again, a stile leading into trees to skirt a garden to meet the B6160. *Just back along the road is the mansion of Farfield Hall, dating from 1728.*

Cross straight over to a gap accessing Farfield Friends' Meeting House. *This enchanting Quaker establishment of 1689 sits within small grounds and is often open for a welcome break.* Joining a driveway alongside, use it only to cross a stream, then at a gate leave it for a wall-stile on the right. *Here a permissive path avoids a dangerous section of road walking.* Immediately bear right on another driveway back to the road, but then take a stile in front to begin a wallside stroll along fields, parallel with the road. At the

far end is a stile by a gate at the start of Lob Wood. Rejoining the road go left and cross to join the footway that starts up. Descend the bend to follow the road past a lay-by and on towards a roundabout.

Friends' Meeting House, Farfield

Bolton Bridge

Before the roundabout take a bridle-gate on the right and cross a footbridge on a stream. A path runs upstream with the River Wharfe, under the modern road bridge to steps up onto the old road on Bolton Bridge. *Prior to its 1994 by-pass the mighty arches of the old bridge supported the busy Skipton-Harrogate (A59) road, and still serve as a noble entry point into the Yorkshire Dales National Park. Only after 59 miles do you vacate it, at another shapely old bridge. The large hotel along to the left bears the arms of the Duke of Devonshire, as indeed do most things in this delectable neighbourhood. A little further, Bolton Abbey's restored station echoes to the sound, smell and sight of trains on the Embsay & Bolton Abbey Steam Railway.* Cross the old road into park-like grounds, and extensive riverside pastures guide you towards the increasingly imposing ruin of Bolton Priory.

Bolton Abbey is the name for the tiny village whose showpiece is more correctly the priory. The imposing ruin dates from 1154, built by Augustinian canons who moved to this beautiful riverside setting from nearby Embsay. At the Dissolution the nave was spared, and happily remains to this day to serve as the parish church. Also of interest is the adjacent Bolton Hall dating from the 17th century, while up on the main road are a Post office, shop, tearooms, bookshop, and a large and very splendid tithe barn.

River Wharfe at Bolton Abbey

After a suitable exploration cross the wooden footbridge for a first taste of the river's eastern bank. *Most of the ensuing miles to Barden Bridge are on permissive paths within the Bolton Abbey estate.* Take the main path slanting up the bank, and ignoring others it rises to meet a wall at the top, then advances on into woodland. The splendid path runs high above the river before it drops to meet a narrow road. A few strides further it fords Pickles Beck, though dry feet can be retained by using a footbridge just upstream. On the other side a gate/stile return you to the river to quickly arrive at a bridge crossing to the Cavendish Pavilion, gateway to Strid Wood. *Here are refreshments and an estate shop.*

Strid Wood is a hugely popular riverside habitat, where man and nature appear to co-exist with little difficulty. A splendid path

network was laid out during the 19th century by the Rev William Carr, who spent over 50 years at the priory church: it has been well maintained ever since. On entering Strid Wood simply remain on the main carriageway to approach The Strid, which cannot be missed. An information panel and seats just before it see the path continue, but firstly a few strides' detour is required to view the spectacle. *Here is the focal point of the wood, as the Wharfe is forced through a gritstone channel of great depth. Lives have been lost in attempts to leap the foaming waters.*

River Wharfe at The Strid

Barden Bridge

The continuing main path slants left to double sharply back along the wood top: however, at the first hairpin a direct path slants right to rise to meet the upper path. As it drops back to the river remain by the bank, soon leaving the wood to gain a stone aqueduct. *This carries water from Nidderdale's reservoirs to Bradford's taps.* Cross to resume to Barden Bridge. *This iconic 17th century structure bears a tablet recording its restoration by Lady Anne Clifford.*

*A detour over the bridge leads up to the ruins of **Barden Tower**. A hunting lodge of the Cliffords of Skipton Castle, it boasted two famous residents from that family. Henry the 'shepherd' Lord came in 1485, being raised in the Cumbrian fells until the end of the Wars of the Roses. Up to his death in 1523 he preferred Barden's peace and the company of the canons of Bolton to the splendour of Skipton. He also had the adjacent chapel (now a restaurant) built. The indomitable Lady Anne restored the tower in 1659 and spent much of her final years here.*

River Wharfe at Appletreewick

The Dales Way resumes on the east bank, and from the parking area a path runs by the river, soon rising to drop to a stile as the road climbs away. The Wharfe is faithfully hugged until the path is forced up by the inflowing Fir Beck onto the road at Howgill. *This scattered hamlet sits in the shadow of the steep flanks of Simon's Seat.* On crossing the road bridge the path heads straight back to the river through a pasture locked between water and wood. *The river scenery hereabouts is of a particularly high order, and this corner has long been a favourite haunt of canoeists.* The Wharfe is again shadowed close as you emerge from woodland to pass beneath Appletreewick. *Access is by an enclosed path by a campsite at the end of the village.*

Wharfedale between Appletreewick and Burnsall

Appletreewick has several claims to fame besides its delightful name. Three halls, two pubs and a tiny church sit amongst a fine assortment of cottages. All stand on or about the narrow road wandering through the village, from three-storey High Hall at the top to Low Hall with its gabled porch at the very bottom. Probably the oldest however is the curiously named Mock Beggar Hall, a fine little edifice. The Craven Arms takes its name from the family of William Craven, a Dick Whittington character who found fortune in London, being Lord Mayor in 1611. Not forgetting his beginnings he was a worthy local benefactor, founding Burnsall's grammar school in 1602. A new addition is a remarkable 21st century cruck barn, the first in the Dales for probably 300 years! The New Inn, meanwhile, achieved national fame in the 1970s thanks to the enterprising no-smoking policy of the then landlord. Beyond Appletreewick the river makes a big swing left, and you are deflected right by a wall to the farmyard at Woodhouse, a 17th century manor house. When its drive turns right to join the road, go straight ahead to a footbridge on Barben Beck, and on again to a stile. The river is rejoined and soon leads to Burnsall, omitting a final loop to cross the last field to a stile at the bridge.

Burnsall boasts a setting of near perfection, with bridge, green, maypole, river, inn, church and cottages fusing together into an unforgettable Wharfedale scene. High above, the steep wall of Burnsall Fell is a bold backdrop tumbling from Barden Moor. St Wilfred's dates largely from the 15th century, with a Norman font and a novel lych-gate. Next door to it is the school founded in 1602 (see Appletreewick) as a very early grammar school. Along with the Red Lion Inn, a tearoom, a kiosk and a shop, the Devonshire Fell Hotel overlooks the village from under the moor.

BURNSALL TO BUCKDEN

DISTANCE 14 miles (22¹2km)   ASCENT 850ft (260m)

ORDNANCE SURVEY MAPS
1:50,000
Landranger 98 - Wensleydale & Upper Wharfedale
1:25,000
Explorer OL2 - Yorkshire Dales South / West
Explorer OL30 - Yorkshire Dales North / Central

This glorious expedition through the heart of Wharfedale is composed of three distinct sections. Classic riverside paths connect famous huddled villages, but form only the outers of a sandwich whose filling is a meaty one, an unforgettable, easy upland traverse between limestone ledges. If the weather is kind, then extensive views will be enjoyed across the rolling Dales from the comfort of luxuriant green turf. After this sumptuous feast the more down-to-earth but equally important refreshments of Kettlewell await.

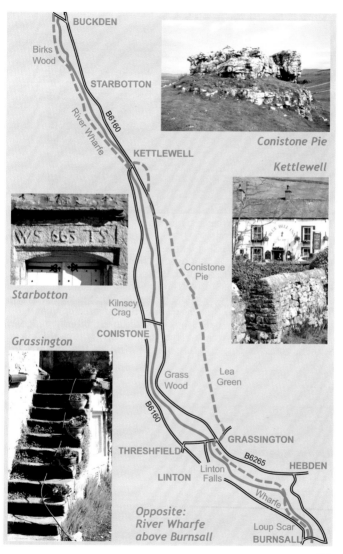

BUCKDEN

Birks Wood

STARBOTTON

River Wharfe

B6160

KETTLEWELL

Conistone Pie

Kettlewell

WS 665 TSI

Starbotton

Kilnscy Crag

CONISTONE

Conistone Pie

Grassington

Grass Wood

Lea Green

B6160

GRASSINGTON

THRESHFIELD

B6265

HEBDEN

LINTON

Linton Falls

Wharfe

Opposite: River Wharfe above Burnsall

Loup Scar

BURNSALL

Rejoin the River Wharfe by turning down between the Red Lion and the bridge, and follow a firm path upstream. It soon sees the back of the village, passing below the church and along to a knoll above the gorge of Loup Scar, where the Wharfe rushes through an impressive limestone fault. In these spectacular environs the path drops back to the river to run through charming surroundings to a suspension bridge below Hebden. *Erected in 1885 to replace stepping-stones since restored, it spans a wide, calm stretch of river.*

On the opposite bank the walk resumes through a deeply enclosed reach of the Wharfe. Emerging, a loop in the river is cut by striking across a large pasture to the right of the tree-masked

Top: River Wharfe at Loup Scar, Burnsall

Bottom: The weir at Linton Falls

sewage works. *At its access road a direct option crosses stepping-stones to Linton church.* The main route turns right through a gate and along an access road past a fish farm. As it climbs through a bend, a stile on the left sends a path back towards the Wharfe opposite Linton church. A couple of fields further, the footbridge at Linton Falls is reached. *Here the Wharfe enjoys a rare moment of anger as it tumbles over limestone ledges, a foaming sight in spate. Houses on the opposite bank replaced a large mill demolished in the 1980s.*

To visit Grassington National Park Centre turn up the walled footway on the right. Without crossing the bridge the Dales Way resumes upstream: in contrast to the turbulent falls, the river flows wide and calm between two weirs. Rising a little away from the river after an intervening wall, the way advances on to become enclosed beneath a terrace of houses at Grassington Bridge. Cross the road and turn right up the footway for the village centre, the Square being up to the left when the main road swings sharp right.

Grassington is 'capital' of Upper Wharfedale, a thriving community with a good range of facilities. The cobbled square is focal point for many hidden corners worthy of leisurely exploration. Grassington boasted an 18th century theatre and a 19th century lead mining industry of which its moor still holds much evidence. Buildings of character include the Old Hall and the former Town Hall-cum-Devonshire Institute. Here also is a folk museum and the headquarters of the National Park and the Upper Wharfedale Fell Rescue organisation. *Popular annual events include the cultural feast of Grassington Festival in late June, and colourful Dickensian Saturdays in Advent.*

The path above Lea Green

From the Square head up the main street past the Devonshire Hotel, and at the crossroads by the Town Hall go left on Chapel Street. Part way along, look out for Bank Lane turning off right. This climbs away and swings left as a walled track. On reaching some stables, take a small gate on the left and cross the field to a wall-stile. Drop left to another stile onto a track, and ignoring a stile ahead turn right on the quickly fading track, crossing to a slender gap-stile at the far end. *The next enclosure is the site of a medieval village, with some grassy embankments discernible.* Curve left as far as a stile in the far wall, behind which a further stile admits to Lea Green. *These spacious pastures were the site of a vast prehistoric field system, its rectangular mounds best revealed in the low light of evening.*

Crossing another path and then quickly a wider one, yours rises gently to join a green track heading your way. A little further, a left fork is ignored, and at the brow a near-parallel wall is seen to the right. Your path joins it beyond some outcropping limestone, when you cross to a stile just short of the corner. Head away to a bridle-

gate beyond an island outcrop and then rise to a stile, continuing up past further outcrops to a huge limekiln. At a stile just beyond, level pastures precede a short pull to the head of Conistone Dib. *Boasting outstanding limestone features, this dry valley leads down to the village of Conistone.*

Pavement above Conistone Dib

Ignore the stile and take the briefly enclosed way to its right to emerge onto a broad track. Cross straight over and head off below a long scar which supports a superb limestone pavement. A stile is soon

Kilnsey Crag from north of Conistone Pie

reached under the knoll of Conistone Pie. *This iconic little sentinel is visible from many parts of the upper dale. From a distance it resembles a man-made tower, but closer inspection reveals natural limestone architecture boasting a marvellous panorama across the trough of Wharfedale to Kilnsey Crag and Littondale.* Beyond Conistone Pie the Way soon traverses a limestone shelf with scars both above and below. After several intervening stiles, path and adjacent scars fade: go straight ahead to a gate/stile at the plantation corner, and a track descends onto the Kettlewell-Conistone road near Scargill House. *The landmark of the chapel at Scargill House, a Christian retreat and conference centre founded in 1959, blends surprisingly well into its setting.*

Turn right past the Scargill House driveway, then after a couple of kinks in the narrow road take a bridle gate on the right. *If you can't face an impending barrage of stiles, keep straight on the road to be in the village within ten minutes.* Head away to a gateway then turn through it to commence a fascinating course through about a dozen fields within half a mile. Though faint on the ground, the way follows a near straight wall, more than once switching sides before finally emerging at the head of a narrow green way on the edge of the village. Turn down it to a T-junction, and then right onto a back lane for the village centre.

Haytime below Kettlewell

25

Kettlewell is the principal village of the upper dale, astride a major coaching route to Richmond. Both the Racehorses and the Blue Bell at the entrance to the village would have served weary travellers, and along with the Kings Head, still do. Shops, tearooms and ample accommodation - with a youth hostel incorporating a Post office - add further life. Kettlewell was a lead mining centre in the 19th century, and the beck racing through is lined by delectable cottages which once housed miners. Footpaths radiate in every direction, by riverbank, narrow gills, moors, limestone shelves and onto the heights, of which Great Whernside takes a paternal interest. St Mary's church takes a back seat, with the village stocks and maypole nearby. Kettlewell found additional fame in the 21st century as principal location for the movie 'Calendar Girls'.

Wharfedale above Kettlewell

Leave Kettlewell by crossing the bridge on the Wharfe at the western end of the village. From a gate on the right a track heads away, but instead turn down a path to join the riverbank. Soon deflected slightly away from the Wharfe, the Way runs infallibly on - at times enclosed by walls - through countless pastures. The river, never more than a field's-length away, eventually comes closer to continue its game of hide and seek. The path's course remains largely very clear to reach a footbridge over the

Below Starbotton

Wharfe. *The track across it offers a short detour into the peaceful village of Starbotton, with its attractive Fox & Hounds pub and some lovely little corners with 17th century cottages.*

Don't cross the bridge unless visiting Starbotton, but simply resume upstream. When the Wharfe temporarily parts company the path continues straight ahead alongside a wall on the left: several stiles and gates interrupt the journey. As the river returns a cart track is joined, but as the Wharfe bends away again after passing a barn, this time a path drops down to a small gate to join the river. *At this very point an extremely vigorous stream survives just a handful of yards before returning below ground.* The Way shadows the Wharfe around to Buckden Bridge, largely on a grassy flood embankment. Though the route continues upstream, few will not cross the bridge to enter Buckden village.

Buckden is the first sizeable settlement encountered by the Wharfe, and stands at the meeting place of two high roads from Wensleydale: one comes over Kidstones Pass from Aysgarth, the other is the narrow, winding strip of tarmac that reaches nearly 2000ft on its way over Fleet Moss from Hawes. In medieval times Buckden was the centre of a vast hunting forest, and the Buck Inn recalls this former importance. There are also tearooms and a shop. The village stands high above the river on the slope of Buckden Pike, and swift-flowing Buckden Beck carves a deep defile down from the summit.

3

BUCKDEN TO GEARSTONES

DISTANCE 13 miles (21km)   ASCENT 1100ft (335m)

ORDNANCE SURVEY MAPS
1:50,000
Landranger 98 - Wensleydale & Upper Wharfedale
1:25,000
Explorer OL2 - Yorkshire Dales South/West
Explorer OL30 - Yorkshire Dales North/Central

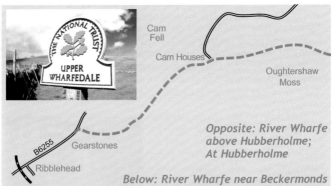

Cam
Fell

Cam Houses

Oughtershaw
Moss

B6255   Gearstones

Ribblehead

Opposite: River Wharfe
above Hubberholme;
At Hubberholme

Below: River Wharfe near Beckermonds

During this section the Dales Way attains its highest point, at 1710ft/521m on Cam Fell, as it leaves the walk's major valley for a brief flirtation with the headwaters of the River Ribble. This is very much a walk of two halves: in beautiful Langstrothdale you positively hug the vibrant Wharfe, leading to a contrastingly bleak upland section that gives the Dales Way its modest *grrr* factor. This is the only stage to end without obvious accommodation: the few options are discussed on Page 8. If keen to get into Dentdale, then the Sportsmans Inn is currently your nearest halt, right on the Way.

29

On joining the road at Buckden Bridge, the Dales Way does not enter the village, but simply crosses to a gate opposite to rejoin the river. A firm riverside path runs upstream until ushered back onto the road, and a half-mile stretch leads into Hubberholme.

*Though barely even a hamlet, **Hubberholme** boasts two famous buildings that are connected by a shapely old bridge. St Michael's church is a gem, with its tower showing Norman traces: a 500-year old oak rood loft is one of only two remaining in Yorkshire, while some pews bear the famous trademark of the 'Mousy' Thompson workshops of Kilburn. Carving therefore - both ancient and modern - dominates the interior of this highest church in the dale. Outside, the sparkling Wharfe runs almost past its very door, and the ashes of Bradford-born writer J B Priestley are scattered here, his favourite spot. Across the river is the whitewashed and homely George Inn in an equally idyllic setting for the first pub in Wharfedale. Formerly housing the vicar, its flagged floors are the scene of the annual New Year land-letting when rent proceeds of a 'poor pasture' traditionally go to the needy. Here also is a busy farm and the impressive Kirkgill Manor.*

The George Inn and St Michael's church, Hubberholme

Cross the bridge to a gate next to the church, where a driveway climbs to Scar House. Leave this at once to regain the riverbank. *From here to Beckermonds this uppermost section of the Wharfe is known as Langstrothdale, with its regularly spaced settlements being backdrop to mile upon mile of unsurpassed river scenery. Throughout this glorious ramble, the path cleverly avoids whichever bank the road occupies. Much of the upper dale came into the care of the National Trust in the 1990s.* The way remains clear throughout as it never strays more than a few strides from the Wharfe. En route you cross Strans Gill ravine above a complex cave system.

Between Hubberholme and Yockenthwaite

Approaching Yockenthwaite turn up to a stile, then on through gates above the lowest buildings to gain the green in the hamlet. *All this area was part of the hunting forest of Langstrothdale Chase, and up to more recent times the small community supported both an inn and a school.* Don't descend to the gracefully arched bridge, but cross over the drive to a gate above a diminutive wooded enclosure to resume in the company of the effervescent Wharfe. After a couple of pastures - passing a well-preserved limekiln - the track fades as it reaches Yockenthwaite stone circle. *A modest 20ft in diameter, this compact grouping of some 30 stones enjoys a noble riverside setting seen by few of the motorists on the opposite bank.*

A dry River Wharfe at Yockenthwaite

Seasons on the Wharfe at New House, Deepdale

From a stile beyond the circle a faint path rises away from the river through a wall gap to another stile. Cross the field top to a footbridge at the other side, then through small enclosures to a gate onto an access road at the hamlet of Deepdale. Turn down to the valley road and cross the plain bridge to keep the road at bay. A cart track sets forth up the south bank past lonely New House, and a little further it turns into a field to leave you on a more appealing footpath keeping faith with the river. In more open country the fainter path passes a pair of delectable little waterfalls before reaching a footbridge and ford at the corner of Greenfield Forest.

Cross to the farm buildings of Beckermonds. *These preside over the meeting of Oughtershaw and Greenfield Becks - the creation of the River Wharfe, no less. This confluence below Beckermonds Bridge is well seen from your approach to the footbridge, a charming spot. Each beck has already covered some mileage to provide a fair volume of water for the Wharfe's creation.* An enclosed way then rises onto Beckermonds' access road. Turn right to bridge Oughtershaw Beck for the short climb to the valley road, from where a mile of road walking now ensues. After a stiff pull the road runs pleasantly on past secretive Oughtershaw Hall and into the scattered hamlet of Oughtershaw.

Oughtershaw Beck at Beckermonds

    Oughtershaw is the first - or in your case last - settlement of any size in Wharfedale. Although more than 1100ft/335m up its setting is far from exposed, being secreted in a sheltered retreat above Oughtershaw Beck. Two unassuming stone memorials to Queen Victoria record her Golden Jubilee of 1887 and her Diamond Jubilee ten years later. From here the road climbs to almost 2000ft/600m on Fleet Moss before descending to Wensleydale. After the last buildings the road turns to climb again, but here continue straight ahead along an access road. It leads past Nethergill and ends at the substantial farm of Swarthghyll. *Nethergill has been revived in recent years as a traditional hill farm with an admirably sustainable ethos. Both farms currently provide accommodation.*

Oughtershaw

At Swarthghyll keep left of the buildings and pass along the front of a modern barn at the end to enter a rough pasture. An intermittent wallside path maintains the same course

Dales Way summit on Cam High Road

through several such pastures, with the lonely outpost of Cam Houses on the slope ahead. *A 'champagne moment' comes with the appearance of mighty Ingleborough, which is to remain in your sights for several miles.* When the wall turns uphill a fence takes over, and a better path advances on, now with a wall on your right to pass a small barn to reach roofless Breadpiece Barn. From a stile to its right make the short pull to Cam Houses, the path slanting right across two pastures before merging into a level track running to the cluster of buildings. *Isolated Cam Houses provides the highest buildings encountered on the walk, looking out across vast miles of bleak Pennine terrain. These uplands of Oughtershaw Moss and Cam Fell have not been improved by a dark cloak of forestry.*

From the stile into their midst, take a gate after the first house and go left above the adjacent bunkhouse towards the access road descending steeply from the right. Before it, however, bear left above a modern barn and an old house to a gate by a final

Ribblehead Viaduct

barn at the end. A short green way leads out into rough pasture. Ignoring the grassy track ahead, take a thinner path rising right towards the top corner of Cam Woodlands. *Towards the top, the dignified profile of Penyghent slots into place to the south.* A stile admits to the edge of the plantation, and 'waymarked' trees point the crude path through the top corner to emerge onto a firm track at the top. A path rises away to a parallel fence above, which is followed left to a stile. The path resumes its climb to a beckoning guidepost and cairn, where you join the broad track of the Cam High Road, at 1710ft/521m the summit of the Dales Way.

At this major junction you encounter the Pennine Way as well as its more recent shadow route, the Pennine Bridleway. The Cam High Road traces a Roman road linking Ingleton and Bainbridge, and was also a packhorse route. Resume left on a gentle decline of over a mile to another guidepost and junction at 1437ft/438m on Cam End. *Surrounded by high country, this excels as a wilderness viewpoint in the heart of the Dales. Directly ahead, Whernside has now joined its Three Peaks partners, while also already in view is Ribblehead's celebrated viaduct on the Settle-Carlisle line.* As the Pennine Way turns left for Horton keep straight on, commencing a steeper descent. At the foot of the fell, Gayle Beck (the infant River Ribble) is crossed by high footbridge or ford. Cross to a stile (note the old Ingleton boundary stone by the gate) and up to the B6255 Ingleton-Hawes road. Go left just as far as Far Gearstones. *Gearstones, just beyond, was an inn astride the old coaching route from Lancaster to Richmond: an old milestone survives. The Station Inn with its bunkhouse and adjacent railway station at Ribblehead are a long mile further along this road.*

Ingleborough from near Gearstones

GEARSTONES TO SEDBERGH

DISTANCE 14½ miles (23km)
ASCENT 900ft (275m)

ORDNANCE SURVEY MAPS
1:50,000
Landranger 98 -
Wensleydale & Upper Wharfedale
1:25,000
Explorer OL2 -
Yorkshire Dales South/West
Explorer OL19 -
Howgill Fells/Upper Eden Valley

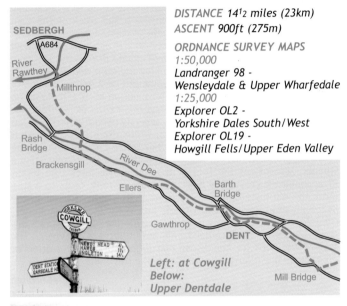

Left: at Cowgill
Below:
Upper Dentdale

Above: the River Dee below Dent

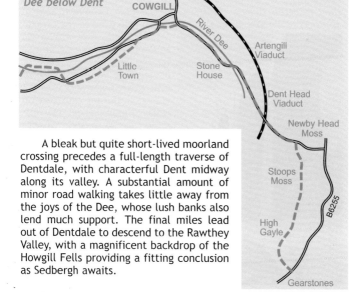

A bleak but quite short-lived moorland crossing precedes a full-length traverse of Dentdale, with characterful Dent midway along its valley. A substantial amount of minor road walking takes little away from the joys of the Dee, whose lush banks also lend much support. The final miles lead out of Dentdale to descend to the Rawthey Valley, with a magnificent backdrop of the Howgill Fells providing a fitting conclusion as Sedbergh awaits.

Opposite Far Gearstones turn up the drive to the houses at Winshaw. Continue up the wallside, and at the top corner the path turns right along the base of the intermittently moist moor. Hold this near-level course until the wall drops away just beyond High Gayle Farm, below. Here keep straight on to merge into a better track rising left across the moor, soon running a pleasant, level green course. Beyond a fence (Yorkshire/Cumbria boundary) an upgraded path continues across Stoops Moss to gain the road at the head of Dentdale. Turn left to commence the longest spell of road walking on the entire Dales Way. *An early milestone inscribed 'S12' refers to the distance to Sedbergh.* Before long the narrow road commences a steep descent to pass beneath the mighty arches of Dent Head Viaduct. *This encounter with the famous Settle-Carlisle line is a fine moment - especially if a train should be coming.*

*The 72-mile **Settle-Carlisle Railway** was completed in 1876, after seven hard years when Victorian endeavour reached new heights to battle against Pennine terrain and weather. It was the work of the Midland Railway, determined to create their own line to Scotland. With more sensible routes running to east and west, they resorted to the challenge of the high Pennines. Logical approaches via Ribblesdale and the Eden Valley led to the central massif from Ribblehead to Mallerstang, and this gave rise to the spectacular feats of engineering you see today, as deep tunnels alternate with tall viaducts. During construction work, thousand of 'navvies' lived in extensive shanty towns: with an air of the Wild West these were lively places, and with little else to spend money on, well-frequented, temporary inns would witness regular outbreaks of violence. Dent Head is the first of two dalehead viaducts and presides over charming beck scenery and an old packhorse bridge.*

Dent Head Viaduct

From here the infant River Dee is accompanied at an easier gradient to pass the drive of Deeside House. *From 1944 to 2006 this former shooting lodge served as a youth hostel.* In the absence of useful paths the road remains your chosen course alongside the swift-flowing and crystal-clear river. *Tumbling over countless limestone ledges, in dry weather it is liable to disappear for substantial lengths.* At Stone House the road bridges the Dee. *This was the site of a 19th century marble works. Towering behind it is the majestic Artengill Viaduct, built in 1875 of this black 'Dent marble' - in fact a form of limestone. One arch longer than neighbouring Dent Head, it strides a steep-sided, rugged gill.*

Above:
River Dee at
Stone House

Cross the bridge to accompany the river to Lea Yeat Bridge, Cowgill, en route passing the very well-placed Sportsmans Inn at Cow Dub. *Cowgill, with Lea Yeat, is a scattered farming community on the banks of the Dee. The tiny church of St John on the Dent road dates from 1838, and is idyllically sited: there is less charm in its yard, however, with the unmarked graves of hapless smallpox victims from the hard days of railway construction. From Lea Yeat Bridge a narrow road climbs up to Dent station, some four miles from the village it serves: perched at 1145ft/349m above sea level it is the highest main-line station in the country.*

Below:
Sportsmans Inn,
Cow Dub

At Lea Yeat Bridge finally forsake the road in favour of a path which keeps you on the southern bank to quickly reach Ewegales Bridge. Here turn left on the narrow back road, passing Ewegales Farm and shortly after, as the road drops right, take a gate on the left. An access track crosses to the farm buildings of Rivling: pass beneath them to run on to a stile into replanted woodland. A path crosses to approach Little Town, which lives up to its name. Its occupants' privacy has been retained by diverting the path down to the right onto a forking drive. Across them bear left up to the far corner (beyond the buildings) to another stile into the second half of replanted woodland. After an old barn fork left to a small gate out into a field, then trace a wallside away to meet another drive beyond a stile. *Ahead are extensive views down-dale, with Great Coum and Middleton Fell prominent.* Head a few strides up it then branch right to cross to a stile, continuing across to meet the access road to Hackergill and Coat Faw.

Turn left along the drive, and immediately fork right on a bridge over a beck to a kissing-gate on the right opposite the house. From it cross to another such gate, then turn right with the wall below a prominent scar. On approaching Clint you are deflected above its confines by a fence, before dropping to a stile and little footbridge to resume with a fence on the left. Through a gate pass along the front of West Clint, following its drive out along a fieldtop. As it drops away leave by a corner stile, continuing on to a drive beneath a house. This leads briefly on to a barn ahead, then

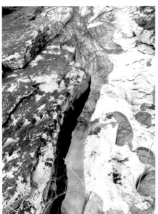

resume along a fieldtop to cross a small beck. Just beyond it pass to the right of a large barn, and from a stile there turn down Laithbank's drive to rejoin the back road.

River Dee at Lenny's Leap

Go left until just past a pair of houses, then take a gate on the right. Drop slightly right to the prominent wooded confines of Lenny's Leap. *This is a tree-girt ravine with a cave at its head: usually dry, the resurgence occurs just prior to meeting the Dee.* Pass to the right, dropping down a few steps to a small footbridge then resume down to the River Dee at Nelly Bridge, a footbridge. *The river is regularly dry here, but not often for too long!* Across the bridge go downstream through a few fields to soon reach Tommy

River Dee above Dent

Bridge. *During this last stage the opposite bank sends forth a whole series of resurgences as sidestreams splash to the surface.*

Re-cross the Dee and resume downstream, but at only the second gate make use of a stile to its left, leaving the river to climb by a wall on the right. *At a mere 550ft / 167m this little brow is a fine Dentdale viewpoint, with mountains such as Whernside, Great Coum and Widdale Fell on parade.* From the top head directly away

to descend to a stile by a cottage, then go right a few strides along the back road to Mill Bridge. Across the bridge take a path into trees on the right. This shadows Deepdale Beck down to its confluence with the Dee, a lovely spot which deserves a pause. The river takes you downstream again, and just prior to Church Bridge you are deflected by a wall to cross a farm bridge, then following the stream right to meet the road at the substantial Church Bridge, on the edge of Dent.

Church Bridge, Dent

41

On gaining the road, no-one will turn down the chance to savour the charms of **Dent**, just two minutes up to the left. Only a village in size, it is still known as Dent Town in recognition of a once greater importance. Today it is an unhurried backwater midway along its own valley. The only roads in and out are narrow, minor ones, a factor which has helped preserve Dent's character. It retains some cobbled streets lined with neat cottages, tearooms, shop, a pair of pubs and a lovely church. St Andrew's dates in part from the 15th century: the tower dates from the late 18th century. The Sun Inn and the George & Dragon are a stone's throw apart, and the latter serves ale brewed just up the road in this very dale. Dent also has an absorbing heritage centre displaying much of local interest. On the main street is a block of Shap granite in use as a drinking fountain, and carved with the name Adam Sedgwick. Born here in 1785, he spent over 50 years as Professor of Geology at Cambridge. One of the earliest and best in his field, he did much research into the fascinating geology of his own back yard.

Back at Church Bridge, take a stile to descend to the river, and resume. *You soon enjoy a fine prospect of Dent village backed by a skyline appearance of the Megger Stones, scattered boulders on the slopes of Great Coum.* The Dee is hugged all the way to Ellers, two miles distant. The only breaks are early on, when the Dee nudges you onto a few strides of road; and on approaching Barth Bridge, where the Way takes a more direct course onto the road. The riverbank path resumes on the other side. *Combe Scar towers over the walk between Barth Bridge*

and Ellers, a colourful hollow carved out of the northern flank of Middleton Fell that has more than a hint of Lakeland about it.

Above: River Dee at Ellers   Below: Haytime in lower Dentdale

Approaching the white cottage at Ellers the field begins to taper, and the Way is sent across to a stile onto the adjacent side road. Turn right past Ellers and its footbridge to begin a mile along the near traffic-free lane. At the attractive corner at Brackensgill a short-lived green way on the right sends a tiny path off to a footbridge and ford on the Dee. Across, an enclosed bridle-track rises to the Dent road at Gate Manor. Almost directly opposite, an enclosed drive

Winter in lower Dentdale

rises away up the hill: when it forks keep left to rise to the farm at Gap. Pass along the front of the house along a short-lived enclosed way, over a field and along the foot of Gap Wood. Enclosed for much of the way, a superb green track soon leaves the trees behind. At an early fork remain on the top path which swings round to the right to a brow at the foot of the long ridge dividing Dentdale and Garsdale. *This is a classic Dales Way moment as Sedbergh and the Howgill Fells appear as you trade Dentdale for the Rawthey scene.*

A bridle-gate admits onto an old golf course: go straight ahead, crossing a track which is quickly rejoined and followed away. This soon heads more steeply downhill, becoming a stony lane to descend into Millthrop. Turn right through the hamlet to a T-junction. *This tightly packed settlement features attractive old millworkers' cottages and a curiously shaped Methodist chapel of 1888.* Go left at the junction to drop onto the Dent road by the River Rawthey just short of Millthrop Bridge. Across, the Way resumes above the river, but few will not head up the road into Sedbergh.

First view of Sedbergh and the Howgill Fells

Sedbergh is a grand little town, and the isolation of this largest community in the Dales National Park has helped it avoid the excesses of commercialism. Ceded to Cumbria in 1974, Sedbergh was previously in the extreme north-west of the West Riding of Yorkshire, an incredible 100 miles distant from West Riding colleague Sheffield. This tiny market town boasts an unparalleled position on the lower slopes of its 'own' mountains the Howgill Fells, and the outlook on three sides is, in fact, of fells. This is the edge of the Dales, and to the west of the town runs the River Lune. In the neighbourhood of Sedbergh three lively rivers end their journeys, as the Dee, Clough and Rawthey join forces to swell the Lune.

Aside from the imposing Howgills, Sedbergh is dominated by its public school. This famous establishment was founded in the early 16th century, with geologist Adam Sedgwick and England rugby captain Will Carling among its old boys. Oldest remaining part dates from 1716 and is now the library. Most other features of interest are on or near the lengthy main street, including St Andrew's church with its 15th century tower, and other parts dating back to Norman times. Overlooking the eastern end of town is the motte and bailey site of Castlehaw. More recently Sedbergh has resurfaced as England's 'booktown', with several antiquarian and second-hand dealers.

Millthrop Bridge (top)

45

5

SEDBERGH to BURNESIDE

DISTANCE 16¹₂ miles (26¹₂km)   ASCENT 1300ft (400m)

ORDNANCE SURVEY MAPS
1:50,000
Landranger 97 - Kendal to Morecambe
1:25,000
Explorer OL7 - English Lakes South East
Explorer OL19 - Howgill Fells/Upper Eden Valley

Below: River Sprint near Burneside

This longest day is one of immense variety as you negotiate the undulating country 'twixt Dales and Lakes. The ever-lively Lune guides you beneath the slopes of the Howgill Fells, before green pastures lead to the rivers Mint, Sprint and ultimately the Kent at Burneside. This no-man's-land between the national parks supports few villages and no refreshment opportunities: ensure everything for the day is carried. A feature of the day is the prospect of fells to all points but south, with those of Lakeland slowly replacing the Howgills. Immediately to the north, Whinfell's ridge rises above the anomalies of the current Park boundaries.

Allow a full day for this section - although route-finding is not difficult, it can be time-consuming. A smart option is to take a semi-rest day in Sedbergh, and just spend the morning walking the section to Lincoln's Inn Bridge, returning the two road miles by bus or lift, then having a leisurely afternoon around Sedbergh's bookshops: you could then return the same way to the bridge the next morning to resume, four miles lighter.

Above: near Black Moss Tarn

Left: Howgill Fells

*The **Howgill Fells** are a compact, well-defined upland range. Triangular in shape, the group is moated by the Lune on two sides and the Rawthey on the other. The fells are named from a settlement scattered along the western base - rather than the obvious choice of Sedbergh - and even this only found its way onto maps in quite recent times. This alone may have helped keep the hills relatively undisturbed: certainly more people gasp at their splendour from 70mph on the M6 motorway than ever set foot on their inviting slopes. The Howgills rise to some 2218ft/676m on The Calf, and provide four further independent mountains. Additionally there are several lesser 2000ft tops and a whole array of lower summits spread along the radiating ridges and outer fringes. They are an absolute joy to explore.*

Having crossed Millthrop Bridge the route takes a small iron gate after a drive on the left. Bear right across the field to a stile into a wood at the end. Remain on the left-hand path above a steep drop to the Rawthey. Soon reaching another fork, the right branch leads through an intriguing walled sunken section. Soon emerging, take the right-hand of two paths heading left, quickly leaving the wood at a kissing-gate. Go left with the fence past the wood corner to a brow by the remains of a small folly. *To the right, Winder (1551ft/473m) fronts the ever-enticing prospect of the Howgills: it will remain so for several miles yet, instilling serious doubts as to the amount of progress being made!*

Keep straight on down the field towards the Rawthey and head downstream past a sports field. The path then rises towards a lone house, running left of it to join a narrow lane. Go left past cottages at Birks to reach Birks Mill in a grand riverside setting. *This cotton-spinning mill now has a more modern use: note also the former mill-race immediately downstream.* Ignoring the footbridge, take a path downstream by the rear yard, initially squeezed between the Rawthey and a treatment works. The Way clings to the riverbank all the way to Brigflatts Farm, interrupted only by an old railway. Approaching Brigflatts the path becomes tightly enclosed, climbing past the rear of the farm to run above a wooded bank of the river to a kissing-gate onto the A683 Sedbergh-Kirkby Lonsdale road.

The River Dee's confluence with the Rawthey

River scenery en route is outstanding, with several additional features of interest. You encounter a delightful confluence with the River Dee before the tall, single-arched iron railway bridge on the former Ingleton-Tebay branch. Immediately after Brigflatts Farm is a glimpse of the white-walled Friends' Meeting House, though with no direct access from the path you must double back along the road to its beautiful setting in the old weaving hamlet of Brigflatts. With a 1675 datestone it is one of the country's oldest Quaker establishments, and is still put to its original use. If open, take a few minutes to savour the calming atmosphere.

The Quaker Meeting House at Brigflatts

Back on the road, go left for a few cautious minutes then look out for a kissing-gate hidden on the right. Follow the fence away to cross a tiny stream, then rise half-left over a knoll to cross to the far corner, a hedgerowed green way running left to reach High Oaks. *The principal house in this attractive residential hamlet bears a 1706 datestone.* Turn right after the main house, then right again to leave by a pleasant hedged track. From a stile at its demise, keep right to a gate at the very far end. A splendid grassy track leads to Luneside Farm, becoming enclosed in the process. After the buildings, leave its drive by a gate on the left, then cross to a fence on the left and follow it away to a stile. Now slant down to trace the River Lune upstream to the A684 Kendal-Sedbergh road at Lincoln's Inn Bridge. *The unevenly arched bridge recalls a hostelry on its other side: only a farm remains.*

Approaching Lincoln's Inn Bridge

The River Lune at Lincoln's Inn Bridge

Cross the road, not the bridge, and go right a few strides to a gate to resume this happy interlude with the Lune. Along the charming riverbank the Lune Viaduct soon appears ahead, preceded by a footbridge on Crosdale Beck. *The red sandstone and metal arches loom dramatically above a pastoral scene, another relic of the Ingleton-Tebay branch.* The way passes under the tall arches before slanting uphill. On fading, cross to find a corner stile opposite, from where a fieldside track heads away with the parallel beck to Low Branthwaite. Cross the farm drive to a stile opposite, then rise across the field to an old wall corner. A path materialises to rise left, soon becoming briefly enclosed. On emerging, ignore the drive to Bramaskew Farm, ahead, and cross to a wall-stile just to its left. *From here Firbank church is seen across the valley. Also regularly prominent is the line of the old railway. High above is unassuming Firbank Fell, a place of pilgrimage by virtue of the windswept corner known as Fox's Pulpit. Here, in 1652, George Fox addressed a multitude and thus began the Quaker movement.*

Lune Viaduct

Continue past the farm to a stile at the end, and continue away down a large field to pass a small barn in a hollow. Keeping left of a wall beyond, a cart track becomes enclosed to lead to Nether Bainbridge. Without entering its confines take a stile on the left, passing the rear of a barn then going left with the facing wall. Use a gate further along to climb to a little brow, then descend to Hole House Farm. Entering its yard, bear left between dwellings to a gate. A footbridge crosses Smithy Beck and a path drops left to a stile. Now cross to accompany the Lune through a large pasture below Thwaite Farm. *Here you encounter the river at close quarters, its wide, stony bank leading the eye to Fell Head, westernmost 2000-footer of the Howgill Fells. The Lune rises 1700ft/520m up on the Howgills, and skirts their base before heading for Lancaster and its own county. This final section is a lovely riverbank ramble, the part-wooded bank rich in springtime flowers.*

A footbridge crosses Chapel Beck and the river remains in close company all the way to a point at the end of a slim enclosure (ignore a stile ahead) where the path bears right to a gate below Crook of Lune Farm. Advance a little further to meet a grassy way, which is followed left to join a narrow road descending to Crook of Lune Bridge. *This beautiful structure curves at each end then inclines to a narrow crest. Dating possibly from almost 500 years ago, it fortunately carries only local traffic - yet is within half a mile of the M6. On crossing the bridge you finally leave the Yorkshire Dales National Park.*

Crook of Lune Bridge

Lowgill Viaduct

Across Crook of Lune Bridge the narrow road climbs beneath the arches of Lowgill Viaduct to meet the B6257. *Arrival here is a minor culture shock, with major road and rail arteries greeting the eye. With a grassy arched bridge beneath it, the fine viaduct (late Ingleton-Tebay branch again) looks over a lovely old Westmorland corner.* Go right and immediately left to a small cluster of houses at a minor junction. Go left on a short drive, past the front of a house and up a narrow enclosed footway. Emerging, continue up above Low Gill until the adjacent

hedge turns left. Here go straight ahead by a line of trees, and at some intervening trees graduate gently left to the field top. From a stile at the far corner remain level, a path soon materialising to run along to join the drive to Lakethwaite Farm.

Head briefly up the drive then take a stile on the right before the first building, skirting the outside of its confines to slant up to a stile at a cattle-grid at the top. Go right on a cart track, and approaching a back road diverge left to a corner stile onto it. Turn up it for only a minute then opt for a stile on the right. *The stile is*

Climbing above Low Gill

an ideal rest spot, a smashing viewpoint with western Howgills, Lune Gorge, Whinfell ridge, and on a clear day, Lakeland fells. Follow the wall heading away, and from a ladder-stile just before a gate, advance to a farm bridge to cross the curving M6 motorway.

Instead of following the track down to Lambrigg Head, go immediately left between motorway fence and farm buildings to a gate/stile onto a narrow road. *Lambrigg Head marks the important Lune-Kent watershed crossing.* Go a few strides left to a small gate/stile on the right, and bear left along the fieldside to drop to a stile and footbridge at the end. Cross an unkempt enclosure to a stile/kissing-gate at the other side, then directly away along a shallow groove to the next stile. A short enclosed way leads to a gate into Holme Park. Advance through the yard along the right side of the buildings to a stile into a field beyond. From a stile at the end bear right across another unkempt section to a bridle-gate, then cross a large sloping field by dropping a little to a stile in a wall opposite. Do likewise in the next field to a stile in a tiny length of wall, then accompany a left-hand fence away over a gentle brow. *This is one of many good viewpoints on this stage, with Grayrigg village around its church. The central Lakeland skyline excites despite its distance, but for now the Howgills remain more tangible. North-west, however, is Lakeland's eastern fringe.....*

Whinfell from Grayrigg

The next stile leads into a pleasant, enclosed path to the environs of Moresdale Hall. The drive leads out over a bridge: instead of following the drive left (or a track right), a path bears half-right up a slope to a parallel drive with the mansion just to the right. Keep straight on a clear path through trees to emerge at a kissing-gate. Remain with the left-hand fence to cross a tiny beck before rising to a stile onto a road. Go left to a junction at Thatchmoor Head, then double back right just as far as a lone house. From a gate opposite, turn right down the fieldside parallel with the road. At the bottom corner a stile rejoins the road to finally bridge the busy west coast main line.

Immediately over, steps on the left send the path away along the fieldtop alongside the railway. *Ahead is an undulating, pastoral landscape, with Grayrigg the only settlement of note.* A footbridge leads through a hedge, and a little beyond a short line of trees, a faint path junction sends the Dales Way down to the right to pick up a tractor track in the colourful environs of a small beck. The track soon rises left, becoming enclosed to swing around to Green Head Farm. Keep left of the farm and head down the access road, but before a cattle-grid at the bottom a gate on the right sends a green way to a gate accessing a footbridge over a beck, a pleasant spot to linger. Cross to the farm at Grayrigg Foot and follow the drive out onto the A685 Kendal-Tebay road. Head very briefly up the verge and cross to the farm road towards Thursgill.

River Mint at Patton Bridge

After crossing a beck leave the drive by a gate on the left and double back to a stile. A short, steep pull leads to a stile above, then a hedge leads over a brow to meet a tractor track. Go briefly right on it but then drop to a gate in the hedge below. Shaw End mansion is well seen across the fields ahead. Head directly away, then bear left to drop to a footbridge on the River Mint. *The Mint's appearance is unexpected but welcome, flowing through Shaw End's park-like environs: note stone-arched Ivy Bridge a few sedately meandering minutes downstream. The Mint begins life as Bannisdale Beck in a deep, unfrequented Lakeland valley, to be absorbed by the Kent on the edge of Kendal.*

Rise up the field behind to a gate onto a delightful hedgerowed cart track, which is followed right towards the elegant early 19th century mansion of Shaw End. As the house is about to go out of sight, take an iron kissing-gate on the left and resume on a parallel track. This runs on to become enclosed to reach two houses. Rise up the front of the second, at the top entering a narrow footway that runs out onto a road above Patton Bridge. Cross straight over and head down the drive to Biglands.

Black Moss Tarn

Go left in front of the house to a stile, and head along a narrow pasture. After a stile at the end the field widens: keep left with the hedge to a stile at the end. Cross the next field with a fence to suddenly arrive at Black Moss Tarn. *Small rocks and rushes line the edge of this colourful sheet of water in its gentle saddle, whose quiet charm makes this perhaps the most obvious place to break journey on the entire route.* From an adjacent stile advance around the northern bank, over a footbridge on the tiny outflow, and soon climb away with a line of hawthorns towards a pylon on the brow. *This knoll gives a marvellous upland panorama: look back to the tarn making a splendid foreground to the Howgills.*

Descend to New House below, entering its yard and passing left of the house to a small gate. From it an enticing pathway runs for some length before meeting the access road to Goodham Scales. Go left along the road, and at a fork take the gated right-hand option down past Garnett Folds. *Tree-shrouded Skelsmergh Tarn might be passed without notice on your right.* Passing Tarn Bank the road ends with a steep drop to the A6 Kendal-Penrith road. Cross and go briefly left to take the drive to Burton House. Keep straight on through a gate ahead to the rear of the buildings, then left to a kissing-gate out into a field. Cross to the far end, above a marshy section to a ladder-stile down in the corner. Go right with a hedge to a footbridge over the outflow of the marsh and onto a fading track. Rise away with a hedge on your right to a brow, and on through a gate at the end. From it descend half-left to a corner stile, with a wide view of Kendal ahead. Rise to another stile directly above, then follow the fieldside away, dropping to a stile in a short section of wall in the bottom corner. Cross to a nearby bridle-gate and over a simple footbridge to briefly follow the stream before leaving via a small gate. Bear right to cross to a stile onto a road junction.

River Sprint at Sprint Mill

Opt for the lesser road right, and leave it by a gate on the left just prior to the terraced row at Oakbank. A slim path follows the wall away (strictly crossing it at a stile partway along) to drop to meet the River Sprint. Head left along its bank past a rickety bridge at Sprint Mill. *This old corn and woollen mill boasts some spectacular river scenery.* Continue along the fieldside to a stile at Sprint Bridge, and turn right over the river and along the road past Burneside Hall. *Dating from the 14th century this is an excellent example of a pele tower, or fortified manor house. Strictly a defensive measure against border raids by marauding Scots, it is one of many in south Westmorland. Now serving as a farmhouse, there is an impressive gatehouse across a courtyard and a lovely pond too.*

As the road swings left to approach Burneside, an enclosed footway runs a parallel course into the village. Though the Dales Way turns right immediately before entering the village, most folk will wish to break journey here, keeping straight on for the main street. *Burneside straddles the River Kent two miles north of Kendal, and is overshadowed by an enormous paper mill. St Oswald's church has a solid tower of typical Lakeland construction. The pub and shop are assisted by a rare Dales Way chippy. Just below the village the Kent is swelled by the inflowing waters of the Sprint.*

Burneside Hall

BURNESIDE TO BOWNESS

DISTANCE 9½ miles (15km)   ASCENT 1100ft (335m)

ORDNANCE SURVEY MAPS
1:50,000
Landranger 97 - Kendal to Morecambe
1:25,000
Explorer OL7 - English Lakes South East

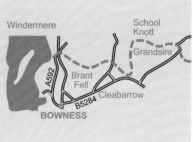

Pleasure cruise at Bowness Bay

An extremely straightforward day brings the Dales Way to its happy conclusion, with ample time to savour the well-earned delights of Bowness and Windermere. Two more very well-defined sections divide these final miles. Firstly the inviting banks of the lively River Kent transport you unfailingly into the Lakes proper, and to Staveley, the only interim village. Beyond here rolling upland pastures take over, typical south Lakeland terrain to guide eager steps towards Windermere's shores. Frustratingly the lake remains elusive almost to the end, and the route skilfully avoids the crowds for even longer.

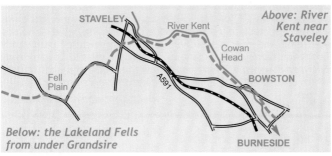

Above: River Kent near Staveley

Below: the Lakeland Fells from under Grandsire

Burneside, 1990s

Leave the roadside path entering Burneside before reaching the first houses. A kissing-gate sees a fenced path off round the perimeter of the mill. Joining the River Kent head upstream past a weir, briefly deflected away to a stile to escape marshy ground. A field is crossed to join the River Kent proper, which is accompanied upstream to Bowston Bridge. Cross the bridge and go up the road to turn right at a T-junction. After a short distance turn right down a snicket immediately after a phone box. Passing between houses you rejoin the river at another weir, and an enclosed path heads upstream, merging into a lane to shadow the river to Cowan Head. *Between Bowston and here you follow the course of a light railway which connected local mills with the Windermere branch line.*

River Kent above Bowston

Remain on the road left of the housing complex to two short rows of dwellings. *Only in the 1990s did Cowan Head's 18th century mill make way for a major housing development which has much to commend it.* At the old houses, now much overshadowed, the road ends and a path crosses to a gate onto the Kent's bank to trace it upstream past a farm bridge. *In this section towards Staveley the Kent is in stupendous form, racing through lush pastures and intermittent woodland. The sparkling Kent maintains its own identity from the slopes of High*

Street to its estuary in Morecambe Bay. Beyond a large barn the path runs through a more rugged, wooded area, then fades when a wall intervenes to separate you from the Kent. Cross the field from a gate to a stile in the far corner to regain the river.

Short-cutting across the next field the path enters a pocket of woodland. *Here, less than 8 miles from journey's end, the Lake District National Park is entered.* When the next wall intervenes at a river bend, pass through a gateway then turn right to a gate, and continue with a wall between you and the river. At the end the field narrows into an enclosed farm lane, and at a sharp bend you leave the track and river by crossing to an adjacent kissing-gate. Follow the right-hand wall away, zigzagging up to another kissing-gate in the top corner onto an enclosed path. Turn right to join the road into Staveley. *This National Park village sees little mention in tourist itineraries, but until its 1988 by-pass, millions were squeezed through, bound for the usual haunts. Of interest is a 15th century tower, sole survivor of the old church. Its various facilities may also demand a brief detour: there is nothing else before the end. Its own river is not the Kent but the tiny Gowan. Beyond Staveley the terrain is very typical of this corner of Lakeland; small outcrops occurring regularly in colourful pastures.*

Turn right on the footway towards the village, savouring a final flirt with the river after passing Sandy Hill Farm. Now cross to the first buildings opposite, Stock Bridge Farm with its 1638 datestone. Head up an enclosed track alongside to use a railway underpass. *The Kendal & Windermere Railway opened in 1847, largely to serve Kendal which was left high and dry by the main line two miles east. The railway created Windermere town, where previously no more than a hamlet had existed.*

River Kent, Cowan Head

From the railway underpass opt for the right-hand of the twin tracks branching away. Remaining with the wall, a small path runs to Moss Side, where a stile puts you among the buildings. Go out along the drive to join the Crook road out of Staveley. Turn left to bridge the by-pass (A591), and very quickly take a branch right onto the old road. Go up this, briefly, then bear right up the drive to Field Close. Pass left of the upper house to a gate, then a grassy way climbs a field to a kissing-gate. *Fine views now look back over the village to the fells of Kentmere and back to the Howgill Fells.*

A pull up the outside of a bluebell wood leads to a gate on the brow, from where a track goes away to join an unfenced minor road opposite New Hall Farm. Go right on this traffic-free back road, which climbs steeply to a brow before descending to a T-junction. *The brow affords a classic view west to the peaks above Langdale, with Scafell Pike and Great Gable also peeking through. The only signs at the road junction are for the Dales Way footpath.* Turn right past Fell Plain and steeply uphill again, then near the top go left along a welcoming bridleway between walls. *From the road-top there is a pleasing view back over the Underbarrow area towards the limestone cliffs of Scout Scar above the Lyth Valley.*

Colourful landscape at Fell Plain

At the terminus of the green lane take a gate on the right (not in front) and follow a sketchy track in the same general direction, bearing steadily away from the wall. From a gateway at the end the track soon swings right to skirt the edge of a small plantation. At its corner when the bridleway goes right, your green way keeps straight on, curving left down to a kissing-gate in a wall, and faintly on between gorse with Crag House ahead. Keep on to a stile by a gate, from where an embanked green way climbs to Crag House. *En route, a not insubstantial spring tires of daylight within yards: the shortest beck encountered just prior to the largest lake.*

An intriguing spring at Crag House

From the gate turn up beneath the large modern barn, but as the track turns in to the farm, remain on the wallside beneath a rocky knoll to a gate in the corner. Descend the fieldside to swing left to a kissing-gate onto a back road in front of Outrun Nook. Go right along the road for a minute then branch left on the drive to Hagg End. Enter the yard and pass between the buildings, then turn left to the rear: a clear path rises gently away alongside a ruinous wall to a kissing-gate at the end. A delightful grassy path now rises over the pleasant upland of Grandsire to a brow, skirts a marshy area to a kissing-gate, and on past a second, larger marsh.

At the end it rises right to a junction of collapsed walls, a splendid moment as you savour magnificent views of the fells. *The proximity of journey's end can be gauged in this prospect west: at the back tower the Coniston Fells, in front of which the wooded Claife Heights rise beyond the deep waters of Windermere, your goal! And from here it's almost all downhill.* The intermittently moist path descends to a gate in the bottom corner of your present enclosure. *From here a detour to the viewpoint of School Knott can be easily made by doubling back with the wall to School Knott Tarn, from where a path goes left to a stile to gain the summit.*

With thoughts focussed on a successful conclusion, the Way turns left to another gate and descends a track to a T-junction. Go left on a clear, level course past a delightful tarn (see overleaf) to the neighbourhood of Cleabarrow, becoming surfaced to join the busy B5284 Kendal-Windermere Ferry road. Turn right on a short-lived but much appreciated parallel path, rejoining the road to immediately escape right on a surfaced drive to Low Cleabarrow. Approaching the buildings drop left to a kissing-gate, then descend a fieldside to further such gates in and out of a few trees. From another one ahead rise diagonally up the slope, between trees on a brow to drop to another kissing-gate. Cross the next pasture to locate a further one in the facing wall, then go straight over a quiet road and down an enclosed path at Matson Ground.

The tarn at Cleabarrow

At Matson Ground you are deposited onto the drive to Home Farm, crossing straight over and onto a third kissing-gate in quick succession, from where a path runs beneath trees alongside a pond. Soon another such gate puts you onto another drive: go briefly right then take a path forking left into a large field. A path crosses to a small gate in the far right corner, then left to a briefly enclosed way onto a farm road. Cross straight over and along an equally short way. Emerging into a field top, the waters of Windermere appear just ahead! A firm path descends the side of a field, crosses a wide track between woodland and continues down what transpires to be the final pasture of the Dales Way - now Windermere more fully reveals itself. Another stone seat (twin of Ilkley's, remember?) awaits 'For those who walk the Dales Way'. *A substantial portion of Windermere's upper section now points to a skyline of mountains dominated by mighty Bowfell and the more familiar Langdale Pikes at the head of Great Langdale.*

At the bottom of the pasture a gate admits to the terminus of Brantfell Road, which leads down into the centre of Bowness. At the bottom go briefly right, then left along the main road past the church. Purchase an ice-cream and make for a suitable gap in the boats and foraging bird-life: a symbolic end can now be enjoyed by dipping a boot into the waters of England's largest lake.

To savour a more rewarding conclusion, consider continuing on a little further past the boat landings to Cockshott Point: here you can sit and take in your week's achievement and memories. Most walkers in these parts regularly hurry past Windermere without a second glance, possibly showing disdain for this tourist halt on their way to more rugged surrounds. After spending some 80 miles reaching it however, one can easily develop a new respect for the place. Come on, admit it, it's still very beautiful.

Bowness-on-Windermere stands midway along the eastern shore of the lake, facing its biggest island, Belle Isle, and the beautifully wooded Claife Heights. The heart of Bowness is a very compact area, with its bulging gift shops a mere stone's throw from the boat landings. For many visitors this is their first, and sometimes only, taste of Lakeland. The environs of the landings form a colourful scene best appreciated away from the height of the season. Not surprisingly a variety of craft ply the waters, from the basic rowing boat to the busy car ferry which shuttles unceasingly across to the Claife shore and back. A small fleet of rather classy cruisers operates a regular service to Lakeside and Waterhead at either extremity of the lake, and they provide an ideal way of seeing Windermere in its true setting. Of further interest in Bowness are the parish church, a veritable oasis of peace in the heart of the bustle, and also a theatre.

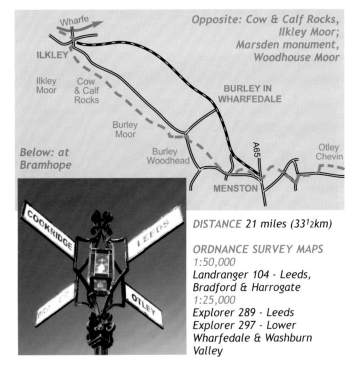

A

LEEDS LINK

ILKLEY

Wharfe

Ilkley Moor

Cow & Calf Rocks

Burley Moor

Burley Woodhead

Opposite: Cow & Calf Rocks, Ilkley Moor; Marsden monument, Woodhouse Moor

BURLEY IN WHARFEDALE

Otley Chevin

A65

MENSTON

Below: at Bramhope

COCKRIDGE   LEEDS

OTLEY

DISTANCE 21 miles (33$\frac{1}{2}$km)

ORDNANCE SURVEY MAPS
1:50,000
Landranger 104 - Leeds, Bradford & Harrogate
1:25,000
Explorer 289 - Leeds
Explorer 297 - Lower Wharfedale & Washburn Valley

The Leeds Dales Way Link was part of the original vision of a long-distance route emanating from the urban West Riding, and it is a surprisingly attractive walk given its beginnings in a major city. Its length might be something of a pitfall, and so the mid-point of Bramhope would make an ideal place to split it over two days, with accommodation and also bus links with Leeds.

66

The Leeds Link begins at the Marsden Monument on Woodhouse Moor, a good mile from the city centre. From the station cross City Square and head up Park Row to The Headrow, opposite the Town Hall. Turn right as far as Albion Street, then left up there and on past the Merrion Centre and Metropolitan University to rise up Woodhouse Lane past Leeds University. The monument occupies the first true patch of green on Woodhouse Moor, immediately after the last buildings of the university.

Victoria Monument, Woodhouse Moor

The statue of H R Marsden was erected in 1878, though this Victorian worthy is overshadowed by a grander monument to Queen Victoria across the road. This is also the start point of the Meanwood Valley Trail, with which your route is initially coincident. Woodhouse Moor was springboard for a Parliamentarian assault on Leeds in 1643. Join Raglan Road to the right of the green sward, and follow it down past red-brick Harrison's Almshouses. Bear left at the junction and keep on this road to a T-junction. Go right here to a crossroads with Woodhouse Street, now leaving Woodhouse Moor. Cross straight over and along the red-brick suburbia of Delph Lane. Remain on here to an abrupt finish at Woodhouse Ridge, where you are suddenly confronted by a deep, wooded cleft, a remarkable landscape so near the centre of a major city.

Turn left on the broad upper path, remaining on it largely in the company of a tall wall on the left. When the wall finally turns away, take the level, central path in front. This contours across a grassy bank and back into trees. Cross a descending path and resume, soon passing the backs of houses to emerge onto Grove Lane (B6159). Cross straight over and along a surfaced path. This runs between red-brick houses of varying age and past a lily-fringed pond with Meanwood Beck to your right and more housing to emerge onto another road. Cross and head along Highbury Lane opposite: at the end a path runs on to a mill conversion. Towards the end go left up a short cobbled snicket past a former millpond to meet a rough road-end. Go right on another snicket which runs between allotments, broadening at the end to approach an urban street. Just before it, turn right over a slab footbridge (not an earlier broader one) on a mill-cut with old sluice gates still in place. A flagged path winds round past a derelict cricket club, and having crossed the adjacent stream, take a wall-gap into Meanwood Park.

Head on through the spacious park, with Meanwood Beck on the left. A firmer path forms at a cross-paths and runs to meet the stream: cross the second double slab bridge and resume upstream to an arched bridge. Across it go left to emerge onto a rough road by garages beneath the stone terrace of Hustlers Row. Go left just a few strides on the track and cross a footbridge over the stream. A few strides further, turn right off the broader path onto one heading upstream. The path soon rises to a mill-cut, following it right through the trees. When cut and stream join, take the footbridge over the latter. Advance to a broader path and go left to a gateway out of the trees. The path runs left along the fieldside outside the wood into the most 'open' country so far, giving a very pleasant walk upstream onto Parkside Road.

Meanwood Beck

Cross the road and bridge to rise towards the Leeds ring-road (A6120). Just short of it, turn right down a broad path which runs parallel with but screened from the road by a tall hedgerow before turning through an underpass. The path heads away from the other side, rejoining the stream of yore, now as Adel Beck. Soon the trees of Scotland Wood are entered by the scant remains of a mill. Keep to the left-hand, upper, wood-edge path for some considerable time, remaining on the main path rising left to run pleasantly on to a fork just short of a stone-built aqueduct. Here bear right, crossing the valley floor in company with the aqueduct. *The Seven Arches Aqueduct supplies Leeds from Eccup Reservoir.*

Across, take the main path bearing left to rise away on the other side. This runs on, rising a little to reach a sidestream just after a cross-path. *Easily missed, just before, is an ancient spring known as the Slabbering Baby, a small, stone carved fountain head.* Across the bridge on the stream the path climbs to a circular pond. Take the right-hand path rising slightly away, running grandly on again. Keep left at the edge of a cricket field, still in woodland to emerge at a clearing with picnic tables. Bear left on a firm, broader path. *Easily missed, again, to the right are the gritstone outcrops of Adel Crag.* The path soon reaches a parking area and a road.

At Adel Crag

Cross to a bridleway slanting up a heath-like pasture. Ignoring lesser forks, keep left on a thinner path to cross to a gateway at the edge into a field. *Suddenly the urban fringe woodland of Leeds is traded for open fields.* The path curves right along the fieldside, becoming enclosed in the corner. It runs pleasantly on past Headingley Golf Course to emerge onto a road. Cross over and along a short-lived rough road. Keep on the golf fieldside path to a corner stile. *Ahead are plantations enshrouding Eccup Reservoir.*

Descend another fieldside to a stile at the end, and turn sharp left over a gentle brow alongside a fence to a plantation corner. An enclosed path descends its side to a dip, then with a good view of the reservoir climb a field centre to a hedge corner and on to join Eccup Moor Road. Turn right towards Eccup. *This scattered farming settlement occupies a quintessential rolling landscape between Leeds and the Wharfe Valley.* In a dip take a narrow road left to rise onto another road, and keep on this (ignore a left branch) to a junction with Eccup Lane. With Brookland Farm opposite, go right just a few paces to enter the spacious farmyard. *The New Inn can be seen two minutes along the road. If detouring, the route can be rejoined by a stile before the farm, crossing a small paddock side to another stile to pick up the main route.*

Eccup Reservoir

In the farmyard bear right to a wall leading to a gate left of a large barn, and head away on the fieldside. A track runs to a gate/stile at the end. A thin path then winds round the left side of a field to a corner stile, and on

again to a similar stile. From this turn sharp right to a brow. *This reveals the promised land of the Wharfe Valley; principal features are Almscliff Crag, Norwood Edge above the Washburn Valley, Arthington church, and the long Arthington Viaduct on the Leeds-Harrogate line. You are also likely to observe Red kites wheeling overhead, after hugely successful releases on the Harewood estate.*

Descend a couple of fieldsides towards Bank Side Farm, through a gate/stile onto a track just above it. Don't drop to the farm, but turn left on the track beneath a ramshackle barn. *You now join the route of the Ebor Way.* Beyond the gate/stile just ahead, your way becomes a grassy track, regaining height to run unfailingly along, enjoying a narrow, enclosed spell before opening out at Bank Top. Follow its drive out onto a road. Cross to a gate and head away along the fieldside to a gate in a dip. Bear left across the field to a stile just past a pond, and from a stile just behind, bear right up the fenceside to a corner stile. An enclosed path soon crosses to the right onto a suburban road on the edge of Bramhope, which is traced its full length to meet the A660 Leeds-Otley road. *Note the preserved milestones on either side which feature furlongs.*

Old milestone, Bramhope

Cross and head along Breary Lane, which runs on as Eastgate into the centre of Bramhope. *Focal point is a splendid old roadsign, while the Fox & Hounds pub has a 1728 datestone. A chippy is also well placed.* Leave by heading straight on again on Old Lane, as far as the last

house. Here a path strikes off right, a splendid enclosed way that emerges onto a brow. Bear left along this broadest of ridges, with a crumbling wall on the left. Pass through an old gateway to be joined by a slightly sturdier wall on the left. When this turns away at another gateway, bear right across a small field to a wall corner. *A gritstone platform makes a super vantage point for the Wharfe Valley.* From the stile the way heads along the fieldside towards housing, becoming enclosed to emerge onto the A658 Bradford-Harrogate road above Pool Bank.

In Chevin Forest Park

Cross with extreme caution and take a rough road heading away just to the left, past houses. This becomes an inviting green way, then a firmer track to enter Chevin Forest Park. Advance along the wood-top path to meet a broad track. Go right, soon descending quite steeply, ignoring branches, to approach a wall corner. The main path curves down to the left, while a nicer footpath drops by the wall to a path junction in front of some ponds. Go left to rejoin the broad track, which runs an unfailing course through the plantations: ascending gently then levelling, it runs on past more open surrounds to Shawfield car park. *A weekend tearoom stands just up the road.*

Without joining the road take a firm bridleway to the right of the car park, winding down the wood edge to emerge onto East Chevin Road. Cross and head away past Danefield House along the rough Miller Lane. Steadily rising, when it swings sharp left take a gate right onto Beacon Hill Moor, on the edge of Otley Chevin. Advance along the central path which rises very gently through gorse and heather to a wall corner, leading along to Surprise View on the crest of the Chevin. *A bird's-eye view of Otley is foreground to a far-reaching panorama: distant natural features include Great Whernside high in the Dales and Boulsworth Hill on the Lancashire border, while man-made creations include Emley Moor and Holme Moss masts, York Minster, Kilburn White Horse and Ferrybridge power station. This has been the setting for many a bonfire, at one time to warn of approaching danger, but more usually to celebrate notable events. It is also the site of a 30ft wooden cross erected at the start of Holy Week leading up to Easter. The adjacent car park gives access to the Royalty pub.*

On Otley Chevin

The path drops beyond the rocks to trace the crest of Beacon Hill Moor, a glorious stride before the path runs into woodland. Keep on, reaching a wall corner with fields beyond. Remain on the wall-side path as it drops down through trees, keeping left beneath some rock outcrops. Beyond them a thin path branches left to find a stile in the wall, and from it a path crosses the field to a stile onto a road. Turn right down to a T-junction, going left then sharp right to descend to a junction at the Chevin pub. Cross into the car park and down a short drive to Chevin End. Pass right of the main houses, then left along the rear to a gate/stile into a field. Head down the wallside to a corner stile, then down the wall's other side to a stile/gate onto a drive at Holly Croft Farm.

At Chevin End

Go left along the main drive just below, passing a couple of houses, then take a short-lived track down to the right, in front of a garden. From the stile in front head down the fieldside, and in the bottom corner a stile sends an enclosed path parallel with the railway. After bridging a stream you also bridge the railway to emerge onto the A65 Leeds-Ilkley road at Menston. Cross with care and turn right on Station Road to the railway station. *Menston village has grown into an extensive commuterland serving the cities of Leeds and Bradford. It was long best known for its imposing psychiatric hospital, High Royds, which was replaced by early 21st century housing. There are several shops and pubs.*

Turn in to the station to find an enclosed path heading away from this side of the rail footbridge. It crosses a rough road then heads off as a snicket between gardens to emerge onto a suburban street. Cross over and on Fairfax Road, turning left at the end beneath the church on its knoll. Turn right on the main street. *Approaching the village edge you pass, hidden on the right, Menston Old Hall, dated 1653, but known as Fairfax Hall after its connections with a famous family allied to Cromwell in the Civil War.* When the road swings left as Moor Lane, bear right on Bleach Mill Lane. *On the right is Grange Farm, with a 1672 datestone.*

The rough road runs on between houses to become a lovely byway with extensive views. Just before Mill House an attractive millpond sits directly above it. Without entering its confines leave the drive by a snicket along to the left, noting that refreshments might be available here. Beyond a stile is an intersection of paths where a stream comes splashing down amidst greenery. A track continues along the wallside to a stile to approach Hag Farm. A

stile by the right-hand barn keeps the walk outside its yard, a wall then leading away to another snicket onto a drive. Cross straight over to another kissing-gate and head off across the field, maintaining this line through several stiles to emerge onto another drive. This time rise onto the road at Burley Woodhead just two minutes past the Hermit Inn. *This pleasant pub recalls a 19th century character Job Senior, a local rogue who ultimately became a tourist attraction.*

On Burley Moor

Turn briefly right to the foot of Burley Moor at the head of Moor Lane. A gate gives access, adjacent to the old Chapel School. Take the main path climbing alongside a sunken way, slanting generally up to the right, aiming for a lone skyline house. On easing when level with it, bear right as the path treads the well-defined edge of Barks Crag. *Outstanding views over the valley now remain throughout the walk.* The path runs on to approach Coldstone Beck, remaining virtually level until dropping down to cross it. A steeper pull up the opposite slope precedes a resumption of the 'edge' walk, with a wall for company: when this falls away a greater sense of freedom returns.

With the road never distant below, the path runs through the colourful terrain of Green Crag Slack. Some time further, yellow marker posts signify Burley Moor has been traded for Ilkley Moor, and the Cow & Calf Rocks and eponymous hotel appear. The main path drops slightly to run beneath the prominent hanging rock known as the Pancake Stone, then cross a green quarry track and remain on the broad path bound for the rocks: a less appealing rough track comes in, but simply forge straight on to the waiting Cow & Calf Rocks. *These esteemed outcrops constitute one of Yorkshire's premier landmarks, and their roadside location sees them regularly swarming with trippers. On a hot, sunny day the temptation of ice cream will delay the attractions of exploring the rocks, a hugely popular climbing area with substantial rockfaces easy of access. The main buttress of the Cow, however, is so uncompromising that most climbers will be found in the quarry round the back. Below the Cow is its offspring the Calf, whose scooped steps offer an easy-angled scramble.*

From the quarry behind the Cow, a path runs on to enter a small plantation with a much larger quarry site to the left. Emerging via a stile back onto the moor, several paths work down to a wooden footbridge over Backstone Beck, from where a path quickly runs on to The Tarn. Here urban paths materialise, and at its far end one runs on to the foot of the moor, where a road descends into the town. Part way down Wells Road, go left to enjoy a nicer descent through the gardens of Wells Promenade onto the main shopping thoroughfare, The Grove. The station is just along to the right, while the appropriate conclusion continues straight down, crossing the main road by the parish church and descending to the riverbank. A path leads upstream to quickly reach the Old Bridge, where the Dales Way proper awaits.

The Tarn, Ilkley Moor

BRADFORD LINK

DISTANCE
12¹⁄₂ miles (20km)

ORDNANCE SURVEY MAPS
1:50,000
Landranger 104 -
Leeds, Bradford
& Harrogate
1:25,000
Explorer 288 -
Bradford &
Huddersfield
Explorer 297 -
Lower Wharfedale
& Washburn Valley

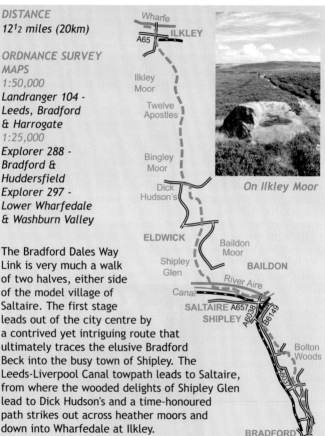

On Ilkley Moor

The Bradford Dales Way Link is very much a walk of two halves, either side of the model village of Saltaire. The first stage leads out of the city centre by a contrived yet intriguing route that ultimately traces the elusive Bradford Beck into the busy town of Shipley. The Leeds-Liverpool Canal towpath leads to Saltaire, from where the wooded delights of Shipley Glen lead to Dick Hudson's and a time-honoured path strikes out across heather moors and down into Wharfedale at Ilkley.

Bradford Cathedral marks the start of the Bradford Link, a short five-minute walk from the Forster Square rail station. Facing the gates, go a few strides left to find a flight of stone steps climbing away, running along to emerge onto a road (Stott Hill) at the top. Go left a few strides then bear right along a setted road (Captain Street), crossing a couple of cross-streets to arrive at Bolton Road behind the Corn Dolly pub.

The Cathedral, Bradford

Cross and go right to the lights just ahead, and just a few paces to the left cross the busy A650 on a pedestrian crossing. Resume rising left up Bolton Road, and at the first chance take the short, setted Lawson Street dropping briefly left. Turn right on it past a small works, quickly transforming into a path through a kissing-gate into the delights of Boars Well nature reserve. A splendid path runs the appreciable length of this natural green corridor, passing Spink Well en route. Keep to the main path which at the far end drops onto Kings Road. Go right to the lights just ahead, and make your way to the diagonally opposite corner. Resume along Kings Road just a little further, then turn steeply left down Bolton Lane.

At the bottom turn right on Hollin Close Lane immediately after Kingsley Avenue. This rough road runs on to a lone house: take a narrow snicket to its right, into open country to rise left with a fence alongside open fields. This levels out beneath a scrubby bank to run towards new housing, merging into a path coming out from them to resume as a part-setted, enclosed way. A little further it becomes surfaced, keeping left of all houses to a gate at the end beneath a steep grassy slope. Ignore both tarmac forks, and rise onto an abandoned road. Cross and ascend the steep pasture to old gateposts, turning left on a neat level path curving around the slope with fine views. This runs beneath quarry spoil to a kissing-gate into a replanted enclosure: take the main path slanting left through gorse to a wall corner. Keep to the better-graded right branch here to slant down the bank to the rear of blocks of flats. Joining a short access road go right of the flats to a road junction at Bolton Woods.

Looking back to Bradford from Bolton Woods

Bradford Beck on the approach to Shipley

At Bolton Woods turn sharp left down Livingstone Road, passing a school, pub, shop, chippy and war memorial. At Gaisby Lane, cross and just a little further, now level, turn right on the part-setted Powell Road. This runs past various motor works on towards the final buildings: just before the barrier in front of them take a path left down a fenceside, quickly turning right to alight onto a suburban street, Poplar Crescent. Advance its full length to a junction with Poplar Road, and cross to find a broad grassy path resuming over open ground past a cottage. With Bradford Beck left and a colourful bank right, this runs pleasantly on for some time. The beck disappears but soon returns to daylight to lead towards a road bridge ahead. Just before it, cross the beck on a much smaller stone bridge to turn right on Valley Road (A6037).

Cross a side road (B6149) and just before the railway bridge a little further, escape right on a path into trees. Running between railway and beck it opens out into a grassy area. Keep to the left path which runs on to rejoin the beck at a rail bridge, passing beneath adjacent arches to emerge onto the setted station approach road in Shipley. *For trains, go left.* Cross this access road and rise a few strides up the main road (A657) to a pedestrian crossing. On the far side go left about fifty paces to a set of bollards, and pass between them to cross to a short snicket leading to the high, pedestrian Gallows Bridge over the Leeds-Liverpool Canal. Across, double back under the bridge and head off on the towpath, past Shipley Wharf where a mix of old and new buildings quickly lead to the classic Salts Mill at Saltaire.

Saltaire was created as a mill village by archetypal Victorian philanthropist Sir Titus Salt, who moved his employees and their families out of the polluted slums of Bradford to this then green field site. Between 1850 and 1872 hundreds of fine terraced stone dwellings were built to house the vast workforce of his brand new worsted-processing mill. The area is dominated by this outstanding piece of industrial architecture, a sight to behold. The village's grid

Salts Mill chimney; Victoria Hall; and Congregational church, Saltaire

system remains virtually intact, along with schools, almshouses, hospital and institute that soon followed. Almost all of these buildings function much as Salt originally intended, and together form a World Heritage Site. And unlike old Salt's day, you can drink here now as well! Beyond the road bridge the towpath takes you directly beneath the remarkable old Congregational (now United Reformed) church, built in a rich Italian style, with a semi-circular front and ornate circular tower.

*The canal at
Hirst Wood Lock*

The towpath continues out of Saltaire along to Hirst Wood Lock. Exactly alongside it, a few steps on the right send a path down open ground to a footbridge over the River Aire. From it a path rises through housing to a bus turning circle. Go left a few paces to find a path striking off into the trees. Running to a major fork, take the left option through the lower part of Trench Wood. Reaching an angled cross-paths, remain on your way which now rises gently right to slant delightfully out of the trees to gain the rocky edge of Shipley Glen. *A place of popular resort since people first escaped city grime, its proximity to Bradford has always ensured a regular stream of visitors. Along to the right, Bracken Hall countryside centre has exhibitions on local history and wildlife, while the adjacent Soldiers' Trench is a Bronze Age double circle with at least 60 stones surviving.*

With an open road just a few strides further, turn left on the gritstone edge above the wooded bank. *Some of the more substantial rocks here attract climbers.* When the attendant wall turns up

towards Baildon Moor, a parting of the ways is reached: the road bears right, while a broad path goes left between bollards to the upper confines of the beck. Instead take the grassy way directly ahead, traversing level ground above a big quarry site reclaimed by heather. Crossing a broader track, keep straight on seemingly inconclusively to the trees. The now slim path runs to the edge of the moor, where a stile sends the smashing little path upstream with Glovershaw Beck.

Shipley Glen

The path is deflected left of barns at Glovershaw Farm and stays with the beck to emerge by a hidden corner onto Glovershaw Lane. *Fading paint on the farm proclaiming 'TEAS' recalls the days when you might find refreshment at any number of wayside farms.* Cross over and straight up the drive opposite to its terminus at Golcar Farm. *Astride a crossroads of old ways, your approach is on the line of a monastic route linking a grange at Bingley with nearby Faweather Grange.*

Don't turn into the yard but advance a few steps further to a bridle-gate at the end of the buildings. From the end of its yard a green way rises between fields, emerging at the top to run left with a wall to the next gate/stile. Maintain the line across a field, rising steadily to a wall-corner. From the gate an enclosed path rises to a gate onto a driveway. This climbs towards Otley Road at Cragside, but halfway up, at a kink, take the left-hand stile and cross the field bottom towards a farm. Don't cross the stile into it, but head up the near side of the wall. When the wall turns off continue up, bearing right to emerge at a stile in the top wall onto Otley Road. Don't leap too enthusiastically onto it, it is quite a busy one, with Dick Hudson's pub just two minutes to the left.

*The Fleece at High Eldwick has been known for more than a century as **Dick Hudson's** in deference to its famous 19th century proprietor. In Victorian and Edwardian times workers from smoky cities made this a place of pilgrimage, coming in their hordes via Bingley and Saltaire to stride out for the moors, often crossing to Ilkley and back in the day. Inevitable breaks for refreshment would be at Dick's, usually on both legs of the journey: the inn served travellers from early morning to late at night. Though the*

present building dates only from around 1900, its predecessor would have served the packhorse trade on this important moorland route. Your author pulled a few thousand pints of Yorkshire ale here in the early 1980s.

Striding out across Bingley Moor from Dick Hudson's

From the pub cross the road to begin a famous moorland walk. Briefly enclosed by old walls, the way rises then breaks free to commence a superb stride across Bingley Moor. A brief paved spell is enjoyed and the path runs down to a large inscribed guidepost. The sometimes moist path forges on through heather, crossing a wall and before long arriving at Twelve Apostles stone circle. *This Bronze Age relic has a dozen stones arranged into a circle 50 feet in diameter. Its well-chosen site overlooks both Airedale and Wharfedale, and across to man's more intrusive ornaments on Menwith Hill.*

Just beyond is a cairn, with the boundary stoop of Lanshaw Lad behind. *Dated 1833, the Lad still serves his purpose, delineating the division between Ilkley and Burley Moors.* The broad path now heads gently down Ilkley Moor before crossing the cleft of Gill Head. Keep on the upper path (left) across the moor, soon dropping

steeply down the western side of Ilkley Crags. *By now you have dramatic views over Ilkley and Wharfedale.* The wide path drops roughly to the cottage of White Wells.

Twelve Apostles stone circle

White Wells is a monument to Ilkley's great spa days. In the mid-19th century many large hydros were built for people to partake of the therapeutic waters: for half a century Ilkley flourished as a spa town of note – the 'Malvern of the North' no less - and the Victorians revelled in the 'healing' powers of its waters. However, a century earlier Squire Middleton built White Wells as a bath-house to enable townsfolk to dip in the pure moorland spring water. In the early 1970s it was restored and opened as a museum and visitor centre serving refreshments. Inside is a deep circular pool hollowed from the rock and fed by a cold mineral spring - though no longer available for a plunge!

On leaving White Wells take the direct, partly stepped path down the last section of moor to emerge onto Wells Road on the edge of town. Head straight down, ideally bearing left to take in a path through the gardens of Wells Promenade, emerging onto the main shopping thoroughfare of The Grove. For the station turn right, but for the true finish, cross and go down Brook Street to the main crossroads outside the church, and down a little further to reach the River Wharfe. Turn into the park on the left, where the Old Bridge, start of the Dales Way, is just two minutes upstream.

Ilkley from White Wells

HARROGATE LINK

DISTANCE 16½ miles (26½km)

ORDNANCE SURVEY MAPS
1:50,000
Landranger 104 - Leeds, Bradford & Harrogate
1:25,000
Explorer 297 - Lower Wharfedale & Washburn Valley

Devised by Harrogate Group of the Ramblers' Association, this first-class walking route links the Harrogate woodlands, Haverah Park, Washburn Valley and the Wharfedaleside moors. The original route ran to Bolton Abbey rather than Ilkley, with numerous anomalies that were dealt with in the previous edition of this guide by an 'Ilkley alternative'. With variations, this has now been embraced as the more logical designated route.

The Institute, Timble

Opposite:
Top - Swinsty Reservoir
Bottom - Harrogate

The Pump Room, Harrogate

To reach the start from the railway station, cross the main road outside the front and head off along a pedestrianised street. At the end turn right to emerge by St Peter's church. Go left, cross to the large war memorial, over another road and down the side of the famous Betty's Cafe. At the bottom bear right to the large Crown Hotel, and the Pump Room stands just to its left.

The Royal Pump Room was at the heart of Victorian Harrogate's spa heyday, serving the celebrated sulphur water to crowds of visitors. It has been admirably preserved as a museum, and the brave can still sample the 'distinctive' tasting water. From the Pump Room cross the road to enter Valley Gardens and follow the left-hand path to a cafe. This area is known as Bogs Field, and a notice advises that 36 of Harrogate's 88 mineral wells are found here. The Victorians piped the mineral waters to the Royal Bath Hospital and the pump rooms and baths of Low Harrogate. The reverse of the notice sets out in incredible detail the chemical combination of four of the best-known wells.

Across the circular garden beyond the cafe, take the main path up the centre of the gardens, soon rising by a wall. The path rises to a junction alongside a war memorial. Bear right on the inviting woodland path to the left of the cross. This runs pleasantly on through Pinewoods to emerge onto Harlow Moor Road. Directly opposite, a broad path heads back into woodland, soon reaching a large grassy clearing. Pass along the right side of this to head back into trees. The path soon emerges to run along the edge of the woodland, with good open views to the right. Passing Pinewood Farm it drops down onto Crag Lane opposite the famous Harlow Car Gardens. Go briefly right and turn left down to the Harrogate Arms.

In the corner below, turn right through a small gate and a path sets off into trees. This runs a smashing course above a stream, absorbing the Harrogate Ringway walk for a few strides before it takes its leave. Down to your right is a deep bowl with footbridges. Stay on the main path rising slightly at a fork to run an increasingly delightful course through the trees alongside an old fence. At the end go through the kissing-gate in front, passing by Pot Bank Cottage and emerging onto the B6161 Otley-Killinghall road.

An immediate stile sends a short-cut path straight down the field to the road at Pot Bridge. Across it climb with care to the brow, and escape left on Pot Bridge farm road. Keep straight on past it to rise to a second farm, The Oatlands. Past the buildings, leave the track by a gate on the right, and follow a cart track alongside a small plantation. At the end take a gate on the left, with another just beyond it at the plantation corner. Outspread ahead is the rolling country of Haverah Park. *Once a deer park of Norman origin, this broad valley maintains a pleasant country atmosphere. Rather more recent is the Knabs Ridge windfarm, which will feature in your view for several miles.*

Follow this wallside along through several pastures, ending as a rough lane to reach Whin Hill Farm. Keep straight on the farm road to Prospect Farm just beyond, and on to the third in this tight cluster, Central House Farm with its unprecedented array of barns. Head straight on again along a firm track, initially enclosed. Dropping to a gate, the track forks. Keep straight on, rising with a wall on the left to run to another fork. Bear left through a gate/stile in front, and the way is again enclosed on a poor, gently rising course between old walls. Emerging, go straight on a faint wallside track, beyond a gate/stile it runs a charming pathless course above a gorse bank, as the old track re-forms at the end.

Valley Gardens, Harrogate

John o'Gaunt's Castle

Passing through a gate the track transfers to the right of the wall, and at the next gate becomes enclosed. A fine green way runs on towards Long Liberty Farm, to join a narrow access road. Turn down it past the farm, and go right at the junction adjacent to the farm. Keep on above a reservoir house and the dam of Beaver Dyke Reservoir, and the way continues as a track into a field above the plantation. Just beyond, a gate admits to the top of the trees and a super green way runs on before dropping towards the reservoir. Just ahead, the dam of John o'Gaunt's Reservoir is reached: don't cross, but continue on the green way ahead. This rises a little before resuming above a grassy bank to cross a small sidestream. From a gate beyond, the delectable way runs on above a memorial seat.

John o'Gaunt's Reservoir

The path at Bank Slack

A knoll crowned by farm buildings across the water is the site of John o'Gaunt's Castle, possibly linked with the old hunting forest. The water tank behind the seat offers a rare choice of Harrogate Corporation's Mild Sulphur Water and Strong Sulphur Water! Resuming, the path comes to a forlorn ruin. Pass to the left to drop down a crumbling wallside to a kissing-gate. Across a low field the path rises to meet a walled green way. Turn left on this to emerge onto the slender Bank Slack, and go right along the length of it. *This historic way retains echoes of its former days. In this charming corner you enter Nidderdale Area of Outstanding Natural Beauty, designated as recently as 1994. The route remains within it until almost in Ilkley.* At the end it narrows into a gem of a green way, running delightfully on to arrive beneath Bank End Farm.

Emerging, take a path slanting left to a stile behind a grass track. It continues across a gorse pasture down to a corner gate. Cross the field to a gate ahead, then advance on the wallside, veering away from it to a kissing-gate ahead. With the cluster of buildings at the Sun Inn on the skyline, bear gently left across a reedy pasture to a wall corner.

From the kissing-gate slant up a garden towards the nearest house. Turning right on the drive out, pass through a gap in the wall in front to gain direct access to the pub, an obvious halt.

The Sun Inn, Norwood

Swinsty and Fewston Reservoirs

Go left on the Pateley Bridge-Otley road (B6451) just to the end of the car park, then turn down a short-lived way on the right. Continue down the wallside to a gate/stile, then bear left down to a bridle-gate into trees. A broad path heads straight down towards Swinsty lagoon. Turn left with the wall to run along the side and quickly join a road at the main body of Swinsty Reservoir. Cross straight over to resume the wooded shore walk, joining an access road going right to the old reservoir house. *Constructed in the 1870s, the reservoir covers 153 acres and holds 850 million gallons.*

Swinsty Hall

Cross the embankment and at once take a stile in front. A stepped path climbs to turn right, passing through a stile into trees. At once take a gap in the adjacent wall and bear right on the broad path, becoming enclosed by older walls. Very shortly a gap on the left sends a path slanting gently up to meet a path junction outside a wall enclosing the imposing Swinsty Hall. *Visible below, this secluded house dates from 1570, its gabled facade featuring a three-storeyed porch and a fine arrangement of mullioned and transomed windows.* At the path

*Winter in the
Washburn Valley*

junction turn left
on a broad path up
through the trees,
quickly reaching the
top of the wood.
Through successive
gates/stiles you rise
through several
fields with a line of
trees on the right.
Faced with the
first open field, rise to find a gate/stile onto the foot of a green
walled way. This rises pleasantly into Timble. Part way through,
turn right on a narrow lane to join the main street.

*This peaceful village sits on a broad ridge descending from the
moors to the Washburn Valley, and the renovated Timble Inn has
long been a ramblers' favourite. Across the street is the former
Robinson Gill Library and Free School, the gift in 1891 of a local
lad who found fortune in America.* Leave on the road rising out.
*Wide views look over great sweeps of moorland dissected by the
hand of man, with the Menwith Hill 'golf balls', Norwood Edge and
its mast, and then Thruscross's great dam slotting into place over
to the right.* Keep straight on past the Fewston junction to a crossroads at Timble Lane End. Cross this brow with care, and a rough
road heads past the few dwellings at Sourby towards a plantation.

*Low House
Farm, Timble*

At a junction
by a covered
reservoir, ignore
the left branch
and take the main
way straight on
into Timble Ings.
With trees on
the right and
scattered pools

on the left you arrive at a clearing: as the forest road swings sharp right, take the more inviting path straight ahead into denser trees. This firm path soon approaches the forest edge, where it swings left over a bridge. As a green way it curves round inside the wall to a bridle-gate preceding one in the wall itself, out of the trees and onto the big heathery sweep of Denton Moor. The main path heads away half-left to quickly reach a cross-paths at a boundary stone under the spur of Lippersley Ridge. *Extensive views are now yours for the remainder of the walk, most notably ahead to the long Rombalds Moor skyline, which will soon feature Ilkley itself at its foot: back over the forest are the 'golf balls' on Menwith Hill.*

There is a brief choice of routes here. The prescribed right branch mounts the gentle ridge to arrive on the crest of Lippersley Pike. A large, hollow cairn is denoted on the OS map as an antiquity: alongside is a boundary stone of 1757. Leave by a path on the left some 20 paces before the top: it drops briefly steeply to head away past a string of grouse butts, becoming a broader track to drop past more butts towards a stone shooting cabin. A little before it, a cross-paths comes in, and the options re-unite. Here turn right on the thinner path. *The direct option advances straight on a green path, swinging right to merge with a broader way alongside a shooting butt. Bear right on this past a couple more butts before it bears left and on to rise slightly to meet a firmer track, with a stone shooting cabin just down to the left. The options re-unite here: cross straight over onto a much thinner path.*

Lippersley Pike

The little path contours on well above the cabin to soon meet a grassy track rising away from the cabin. Advance along this, a gentle rise leading to a brow: ignore the lesser option straight on, and swing left on the main track as it starts a lengthy descent of the moor, with the big hollow of Dearncomb over to the right. Though the way narrows it leads faithfully to the bottom corner: don't advance to the corner gate/stile, but pass through a gate on the left just before it to leave the moor.

With a wall to your left, descend the fields towards Hollingley Farm. Through the bottom corner gate escape the farm's environs by taking an almost adjacent gate and follow a fence away right to approach a deep wooded gill. At the end bear left to a gate/stile, and a green way runs briefly through bracken before doubling back down to a ford and footbridge in the deep gill of Fairy Dell. Across the bridge, cross straight over the track and ascend the steep bank, a thin path forming to rejoin the track on levelling out. Advance towards East Moor House Farm, but as the track swings in to it, take a rougher track bearing right up to an old fence corner. Now go left along the fieldside to a gate onto a surfaced access road. Go left on this through Westmoor House Farm, remaining on this drive through the fields to Hill Top Farm.

Descend the narrow road into Middleton, keeping right at a fork to quickly reach a crossroads. Go straight over and down the suburban Curley Hill. *Part way down it runs by Middleton Woods, which in springtime features a stupendous carpet of bluebells.* When it levels out and swings right at the bottom, take a path on the left down into playing fields. Pass the open-air swimming pool to cross a road, and past sports fields to gain the bank of the River Wharfe. Turn right with it to a road bridge, and for the town centre, go up it. For the Old Bridge, cross the road and continue upstream a few minutes further.

Middleton Woods

RECORD OF THE JOURNEY

Date	Place	Miles daily	Miles total	Notes
	Ilkley	-	-	
	Addingham	2^1_4	2^1_4	
	Bolton Bridge	4^1_2	4^1_2	
	Bolton Priory	5^1_2	5^1_2	
	Barden Bridge	8^1_4	8^1_4	
	Howgill	9^3_4	9^3_4	
	Appletreewick	10^3_4	10^3_4	
	Burnsall	12	12	
	Linton Falls	2^3_4	14^3_4	
	Grassington	3^1_2	15^1_2	
	Conistone Pie	7	19	
	Kettlewell	10	22	
	Starbotton	12	24	
	Buckden	14	26	
	Hubberholme	1^1_4	27^1_4	
	Yockenthwaite	2^3_4	28^3_4	
	Beckermonds	5^1_4	31^1_4	
	Oughtershaw	6^1_4	32^1_4	
	Cam Houses	9^3_4	35^3_4	
	Far Gearstones	13	39	
	Stone House	4^3_4	43^3_4	
	Cowgill	5^1_2	44^1_2	
	Mill Bridge	8^3_4	47^3_4	
	Church Br (Dent)	10	49	
	Barth Bridge	11	50	
	Brackensgill	13^1_4	52^1_4	
	Millthrop	14^3_4	53^3_4	
	Millthrop Bridge	15	54	
	Lincoln's Inn Bridge	3^3_4	57^3_4	
	Crook of Lune Br	7	61	
	Lowgill	7^1_2	61^1_2	
	Lambrigg Head	8^3_4	62^3_4	
	Grayrigg Foot	11^1_2	65^1_2	
	Black Moss Tarn	13	67	
	Burton House (A6)	14^3_4	68^3_4	
	Burneside	16^1_2	70^1_2	
	Bowston	1	71^1_2	
	Staveley (A591)	3^1_2	74	
	Fell Plain	5	75^1_2	
	Cleabarrow (B5284)	7^3_4	78^1_4	
	Bowness Bay	9^1_2	80	

USEFUL CONTACTS

Dales Way Association
PO Box 1065, Bradford BD1 9JY
• www.dalesway.org.uk

Yorkshire Dales Society
Town Hall, Cheapside, Settle BD24 9EJ
• 01729-825600   www.yds.org.uk

Information Centres
Station Road Ilkley • 01943-602319

Hebden Road Grassington • 01756-751690

Main Street Sedbergh • 015396-20125

25 Stramongate Kendal • 01539-735891

Glebe Road Bowness • 015394-42895

Victoria Street Windermere • 015394-46499

Dent

Public Transport Information
Traveline • 0870 608 2608   www.traveline.org.uk
National Rail Enquiries • 08457-484950
www.nationalrailenquiries.org.uk

Dent Head

INDEX
Principal features, main route only